I0754001

To Prevent Or Stop Wars

What Can Peace Movements Do?

To Prevent Or Stop Wars

First published 2016

by Irene Publishing in collaboration with

Institut für Friedensarbeit und Gewaltfreie Konfliktaustragung
Hauptstr. 35, D-55491 Wahlenau Germany www.ifgk.de

and

Folkereisning Mot Krig (Norwegian section of War Resisters' International) www.ikkevold.no

ISBN 9789188061126

Irene Publishing
Sparsnäs 1010, 66891 Ed, Sweden
irene.publishing@gmail.com
www.irenepublishing.com

Layout by Jørgen Johansen
Cover by Øystein Kleven and Jørgen Johansen
The front is based on a photo of a statue in Karlstad, Sweden, celebrating to role women had in the prevention of war 1905.

To Prevent Or Stop Wars

What Can Peace Movements Do?

Christine Schweitzer

with Jørgen Johansen

Translation of IFGK Working Paper No 25

Contents

Abstract

This paper is based on seven examples of peace movements of the last 110 years. It looks at the impact these movements may have had on the prevention or the ending of wars their own governments were engaging in. These examples are:

- Norway-Sweden 1905
- the movement against the Vietnam war in the 1960s and early 1970s
- the movement against the support of the Contras in Nicaragua in the 1980s
- the peace movement of the 1980s against nuclear weapons
- the case of the Women in White in Liberia in 2002-2003
- the movement against the Iraq war in 1991 [a.k.a. 'Persian Gulf War' or Gulf War II] 1
- the movement against the Iraq war in 2003 [a.k.a. Gulf War III]

The main finding of the comparison is that to prevent or stop wars is probably the most difficult objective a social movement may set itself. With the exception of the early Scandinavian case which was a case of successful war prevention, some of the movements against wars impacted both the conduct of the conflict and its eventual end but none of them could be attributed with stopping it alone. Besides this result, evidence was found that the respective movements had a long-term influence on public opinion and helped to raise public awareness on issues of wars and so-called "humanitarian intervention".

However, there was also clear evidence that the respective movements had a long-term influence on public opinion. They helped to raise public awareness on issues of wars and so-called "humanitarian interventions." This, in turn, had an influence on later crises and how governments dealt with them in regard to engaging or not engaging in war.

Acronyms

AFL-CIO = American Federation of Labor and Congress of Industrial Organizations (USA)

AWACS = Airborne Early Warning and Control System (a radar system on a plane)

AWOL = Absent without leave

BUND = Alliance for Environment and Protection of Nature (Germany)

CALCAV = Clergy and Laymen Concerned About Vietnam (USA)

CND = Campaign for Nuclear Disarmament (UK)

CNVA = Committee for Nonviolent Action (USA)

DFG-VK = German Peace Society-United War Resisters

DFU = German Peace Union

DKP = German Communist Party

ECOWAS = Economic Community of West African States

FOR = Fellowship of Reconciliation (USA)

FRG = Federal Republic of Germany (West Germany)

GDR = German Democratic Republic (East Germany)

GPT = Gulf Peace Team

IALANA = International Association of Lawyers against Nuclear Arms

ICJ = International Court of Justice

IFGK = Institute for Peace Work and Nonviolent Conflict Transformation (Germany)

INF Treaty = Intermediate-Range Nuclear Force Treaty

IPPNW = International Physicians against Nuclear War

KA = Coordination Committee of the Peace Movement (Germany)

KB = Communist Alliance (Kommunistischer Bund, Germany)

LURD = Liberians United for Reconciliation and Democracy

LWI = Liberian Womens' Initiative

MARWOPNET = Mano River Union Women's Peace Network

MP = Member of Parliament

NORNONS = Nordic Nonviolence Studygroup

NSA = National Security Agency (USA)

PDS = Party of Democratic Socialism (Germany)

SANE = National Committee for a Sane Nuclear Policy (USA)

SDS = Students for a Democratic Society (USA)

SPAAS = Swedish Peace and Arbitration Society

SPD = Social Democratic Party of Germany

U.S. = United States of America

UNSC = UN Security Council

WANEP = West African Network for Peace

WIPNET = Women in Peacebuilding Network

Acknowledgements

The authors would like to thank their colleagues in the Institute for Peace Work and Nonviolent Conflict Transformation for all their useful comments on earlier drafts of the German paper. In particular, thanks to Martin Arnold, Anne Dietrich, Reinhard Eismann and Barbara Müller.

Jørgen Johansen also thanks the participants at the NORNONS seminar - Stellan Vinthagen, Henrik Frykberg, Daniel Ritter, Jacob Børresen, and Majken Jul Sørensen - for their valuable comments to the manuscript. And to Majken Jul Sørensen in particular for reading his article in several phases of the production.

And last but not least we both give our thanks to David Grant who improved the English of our rough initial translation. As one who had taken part in several of the described movements, he also helped to correct and add to the descriptions of some – an enormous support which has considerably improved this study.

Introduction

This book is the slightly expanded version of a Working Paper published by the Institute for Peace Work and Nonviolent Conflict Transformation (IFGK). It presents the results of a small project that the authors carried out within the IFGK (www.ifgk.de). The study is mostly based on secondary literature on seven antiwar movements that took place between 1900 and 2015. Jörgen Johansen has contributed the section on the conflict between Norway and Sweden. Christine Schweitzer has written the other six case studies.

In the following sections the research question will be described first. After that we sketch relevant information including lessons and approaches that can be drawn from the studies of social movements. We also draw from the study of impact of (international) conflict transformation and from the research on nonviolent uprisings (civil resistance). The introduction ends with a section on methodology.

The following chapter then presents seven examples of peace movements between the beginning of the 20th century and 2003.

The study concludes with a chapter that summarizes the relevant findings and draws some conclusions.

The Research Question

„*We have never ever prevented a war*" was the title of an interview with two leading figures of the German peace movement – the late Peter Strutynski and the speaker of IALANA, Reiner Braun -- in the daily paper „Neues Deutschland" on the 13th of February 2013.[1] This study will discuss if this is in fact the case in regards to what role peace movements have played in the prevention or

1 http://www.koop-frieden.de/ [1.4.2013]

the ending of wars. Here only such wars are referred to which either happened in the country of the movement in question, or wars in which its government was elsewhere engaged, i.e., civil wars or wars of foreign intervention. The study is not about "peace-making" or "peace enforcement" in the language of the United Nations where a third party helps to settle an armed conflict or seeks to enforce its settlement in a third country.[2] It is about those cases where citizens oppose the actions of their own government when that government is preparing or engaged in war.

Are there cases when armed conflicts were ended by citizens? Are there examples where there is reason to assume that without the intervention of a peace movement there would have been war? Or would an existing war have escalated considerably? Or, less ambitiously put, what influence, if any, did peace movements have on the prevention, continuation or ending of war?

This study compares seven peace movements dealing with such objectives.[3] Christine Schweitzer, the initiator of the study before Jörgen Johansen joined it -- had originally intuitively assumed that she had chosen some cases which would be "success stories" and some others which clearly were not. But in the course of the study it turned out that both assumptions were faulty. The first-glance "successes" were multi-layered and less clear than expected. And the seeming "failed" movements had impact though only indirect and limited.

---

2 See Boutros Boutros-Ghali (2002).

3 The study does not deal with movements that sought the ban of certain types of weapons (cluster munition, land mines, nuclear weapons or, recently, drones). The successes of such movements are obvious and not controversial (see Küchenmeister 2010). But they fall short of the target of war prevention.

Lessons From Social Movement Research

The question of impact of social movements is less often asked in the research on social movements than one might assume. In 1999 Guigni stated: „*The study of the consequences of social movements is one of the most neglected topics in the literature*" (Giugni 1999:xiv-xv). This holds true to some degree even until today, 25 years later. Studies of social movements are often descriptive or more interested in the various actors, their connections and networks. Studies often focus on the motivations or biographical consequences of participation in a movement. The problems with the assessment of impact are obvious.

First: What is "success" and how is it measured? Is the criteria for success the achievement of particular objectives that the actors in the movement publicly announced? What other criteria may there be? How to deal with the fact that there is often no unity in movements regarding the objectives (see Giugni 1999)? Gamson calls success an "*elusive idea*" (p. 350) and suggests:

„*It is useful to think of success as a set of outcomes, recognizing that a given challenging group may receive different scores on equally valid, different measures of outcome. These outcomes fall into two basic clusters: one concerned with the fate of the challenging group as an organization and one with the distribution of new advantages to the group's beneficiary. The central issue in the first cluster focuses on the acceptance of a challenging group by its antagonists as a valid spokesman for a legitimate set of interests. The central issue in the second cluster focuses on whether the group's beneficiary gains new advantages during the challenge and its aftermath.*"(Gamson 2003:350)

This distinction is also of quite some relevance for peace movements as the cases studied show even though Gamson was probably thinking of other types of movements. For peace movements, it translates into the divergence between, on the one hand, acceptance of the movement and the sharing of its goals by a (relative or absolute) majority of the population and, on the other hand, the immediate and short-term achievement of its objectives (e.g. the ending of a war and the avoidance of more victims and destruction).

Second: Impact is difficult to capture in complex social processes. It is possible to ascertain change but its causes are usually multiple and it is rarely possible to ascribe an impact beyond any doubt to one specific cause. And if there was impact – can it be attributed to variables that were controlled by the movements? Or are the causes rather external ones, based in the environment or in the particular context (see Rucht 2007:33 and Giugni 1999)? Many authors consider the capacity of peace movements to achieve direct impact relevant to their objectives as limited:

„*Peace movements can bring states to the arms negotiating table, get them to sit down and talk, but cannot make them agree. States are still able to reserve the right, still have the power, to make treaties (or not) with their adversaries. But... the simple act of sitting down to the table puts pressure on formal democracies to reach an agreement.*"(Breyman 2001: 274)

Wouldn't it be possible to simply ask the actors – the politicians deciding the question of war or peace – what impact the peace movement had on their decisions? Theoretically yes, but those who rule usually do not like to admit that they have been influenced by protest, at least not in public. And even if they would respond, it still would be a subjective opinion and no "proof", because actors are not always conscious of all the factors that led them to take or not take certain action.

And what about activists? Surprisingly, peace movements often tend to underestimate their own impact and successes or do not recognize them at all (compare Moyer 1987, who observed the same for the anti-nuclear movement). And all this is made even more difficult by the fact that sometimes the change the movement strive for happened at a moment when the activities of the movement were greatly reduced or the movement did not exist anymore at all (Raschke 1988:388).

Thirdly: It is important to distinguish direct from indirect impact. And intended from not intended impact. Indirect impact is that which had required mediation by others. For example by other political actors or by later movements (Raschke 1988:385). That means that they do not achieve their objective immediately, while at the peak level of their activities, but the intended change eventually takes place because the pursuit of the objective has been continued by other actors.

The difference between intended and not intended impact is one which is well known in evaluation research. For peace movements, a not intended impact or example could be that a peace agreement is delayed because one party to the conflict assumes that the movement to end the war that is active in the country of the opponent will succeed and the opponent will eventually withdraw. (In the case of the Vietnam war there are indicators for such a situation.)

Some researchers of social movements have identified variables that have to be present in order to make a movement successful. Stephen Zunes, looking at the Gulf War of 1991 and referring to the work of the sociologist Todd Gitlin, names the following three criteria:

1. The elites have to divide.
2. People have to feel there is a politically convincing alternative.
3. People have to feel the war is going badly on its own terms (Zunes 2011:360, quoting Todd Gitlin).

Another question is the role that violence plays in a movement. There are two contradictory assumptions to be found. Usually it is assumed that violence harms a movement. But there is also the contrary thesis, based on a study by Gamson (1990) that "*disruptive tactics*" (by which he mostly means violence) may be more successful than moderate actions. Raschke proposed that the question whether violence or non-violence are more promising depends largely on the question what kind(s) of violence are accepted as legitimate in public opinion (Raschke 1988:393; see also Giugni 1999:xv pp).

Schock (2005:157) addresses the related aspect of what he calls "radical flank effects". This is about movements which have a moderate and a radical wing, and that may profit from the radical wing insofar as the demands of the "moderates" then seem more easily acceptable. But there are other cases when movements were discredited because of extremism. The positions and destructive activities of the extremists were not acceptable for the vast majority of the population.

Lessons From the Research on Impact of Conflict Transformation Work

In the last ten years a number of studies have been published that deal with the impact of conflict transformation or peacebuilding and the role of civil society. Without being able to discuss here all debates – not all findings are non-controversial -- a few central findings shall be listed here:

1. One function civil society plays quite successfully in dealing with conflict is to enable and mediate dialogue on the local and national level among the various actors (Paffenholz 2010).
2. In regard to mediation by an external party, there are a small number of international NGOs that offer 'good services' or in some cases even are active directly as

mediators. However, for the large group of NGOs the access to the highest political level is not possible (see Schweitzer 2010:125pp and the literature discussed there).

3. Civil society is not 'almighty'. Most successful efforts to handle conflicts were undertaken hand in hand with other actors, including state actors (Barnes 2007, Paffenholz 2010, articles in Heinemann-Grüder & Bauer 2013).

These findings are relevant insofar as the issues researched here, as they emphasize the importance of communication and cooperation between movements and political elites.

Lessons From Newer Research on Nonviolent Uprisings and Civil Resistance

In the last ten years several studies have been published that compared nonviolent uprisings, identifying factors which made such uprisings successful.[4] Overthrowing a regime is, at least at first glance, a much more radical objective than the prevention or ending of a war. Therefore the hypothesis may be advanced that those factors that make uprisings and revolutions successful would be relevant for peace movements as well.

Chenoweth and Stephan (2011), Nepstad (2011) and Schock (2005) identified several factors as reasons for success of nonviolent movements:

1. Commitment of the movement to stick to nonviolent means. In those cases where a movement did not manage to maintain nonviolence, they failed.

4 A comparison between violent and nonviolent uprisings by Chenoweth & Stephan (2011) showed that nonviolent movements were successfully toppling the government in 53%, the violent ones only in 26%.

2. The uprising is within the country and internationally considered to be legitimate.

3. Large numbers of citizens participate.

4. Attacks from the side of the regime strengthen the internal coherence of the protesters and lead to even more people withdrawing their support from the regime (undermining the power to sanction).

5. Security force members change their loyalty or mutiny. This happens, all studies agree, in cases where the protesters remain nonviolent and do not show hostility towards the military (including not verbally), but approach them as „a part of U.S.". In cases when security forces were seen only as enemies, rather than as potential allies, the chances for the uprising to fail was much higher.

6. Decentralisation of campaigns is often useful.

7. Nepstad mentions two other factors that may lead to a movement failing: conflict within the movement; and division in its leadership.

Another aspect to consider concerns the individual attitude regarding the conflict and the opponent in general. In his dissertation on "Truth Force"[5] Martin Arnold describes the assumptions of three leading protagonists of nonviolent action regarding how they achieved impact: Mohandas K. Gandhi, Hildegard Goss-Mayr and Bart de Ligt.. He summarized[6] his findings as far as they may be relevant for our study:

"*In all likelihood the way in which activists see themselves plays a large role in their success in reducing problems. This is especially true when these are problems that, in order to be reduced, need the cooperation of all people or groups involved. The attitude of the activists to these others, including the*

5 German „Gütekraft", verbally the „force of mercy".

6 Personal communication with the author.

opponents, is essential because it defines the style of communication. The chances for success in reducing the problem are high if – independent of possible hostile behaviour of the others – an attempt is made consistently to break down the opposition and to win the others -- based on things both sides have in common with each other."

As we will describe in the next section the factors listed here have been considered, as variables in the study of the seven cases of antiwar movements.

Methodology

The question studied in this research has, to our knowledge, not previously been approached in a comparative manner in peace research. There are studies of individual movements that *inter alia* ask about their impact. And there are a small number of publications of peace activists - for example by Bob Overy (1988) or articles in the magazine Friedensforum 1/2010 - that discuss successes of peace movements. But they did not focus only on the prevention or stopping of wars, but also included peace movements working on the banning of particular types of weapons, etc. (see footnote 3).

Choice of Cases

Seven movements have been chosen that were adequately documented.

Jörgen Johansen describes the tensions between Sweden and Norway which almost led to a war in 1905 when Norway sought to separate from Sweden. The other six cases have been researched by Christine Schweitzer:

- the movement against the Vietnam war in the 1960s and early 1970s
- the movement against the support of the Contras in

Nicaragua in the 1980s

- the peace movement of the 1980s against nuclear weapons
- the case of the Women in White in Liberia in 2002-2003
- tthe movement against the Iraq war in 1991 [a.k.a. 'Persian Gulf War' or Gulf War II]
- -the movement against the Iraq war in 2003 [a.k.a. Gulf War III]

These seven examples fall into three tentative types:

a) Movements against a war which the activists considered unjust and which their government was fighting outside of their own country (Vietnam, Nicaragua, Iraq 1991 and 2003)

b) one movement that was directed against a civil war in its own country (Liberia)

c) two movements directed against a potential war (Norway-Sweden 1905 and the peace movement of the 1980s)

In the framework of a larger study those cases would have to be distinguished more clearly. But for the limited framework of this study it seemed inviting to look at peace movements happening in different contexts to see if there are indeed differences that can be clearly identified, depending on context variables, in regard to the impact of the movements.

Impact Factors

The table on the nexts pages shows an overview of the main impactfactors on respectively the war, the movement, and the context developments in the societies:

Factor	Assumption(s)
ON WAR	
Duration of the war / the conflict	Movements need a certain time to gather „speed".
Number of casualties on the activists' own side.	The more victims there are on their own side, the more citizens would want the war to end.
Number of casualties on the enemy side.	The more victims there are on the enemy side, the more chances a movement has to arouse moral outrage.
Physical / geographical closeness of the conflict.	The closer the conflict, the more concerned people are.
ON THE MOVEMENT	
Duration of the movement.	The duration has influence on the level of impact.
Participation (the numbers of protesters).	The more participants, the higher the chances for impact.
Unity regarding objectives.	Unity increases chances for impact.
Social diversity of members and supporters.	Social diversity increases chances for impact.
Clear leadership.	Identifiable speakers or leaders increase impact.
Tactical diversity. Especially a certain degree of civil disobedience or other direct nonviolent actions.	Gives energy to a movement and thereby increases chances for impact.
Contact to the government of the 'enemy'.	There may be both positive and negative influence on the success of a movement.

Contact to people in the attacked country.	Such contacts increase the power for impact of a movement because they increase consternation.
Constructive programmes, humanitarian aid	Such work increases the power for impact of a movement because it is widely recognized as 'good'.
Level of violence from the ranks of the movement.	Both positive and negative consequences for the success of a movement are possible.
Support of the movement by other states.	Both positive and negative consequences for the success of a movement are possible.
Support by civil society of other countries, cooperation between peace movements.	At least in cases when the conflict is internationalized (military alliances, „coalitions of the willing"), such cooperation increases the power for impact of a movement.
Degree of sanctions (repression) directed against the movement.	Both positive and negative consequences for the success of a movement are possible.
Casualties within the movement.	Both positive and negative consequences for the success of a movement are possible.
CONTEXT-DEVELOPMENTS IN SOCIETY:	
Divided elites and loyalty shifts in the country of the movement.	Divided elites and the possibility that former opponents become allies are considered important factors for the chances of success of a movement.
Events that can be made a scandal during the war, e.g., scandals of government.	Such events enable a movement to influence public opinion and thereby increases their chances of impact.

Case Studies of Peace Movements

In the following chapter seven examples of social movements that were directed against war are presented. The last section mentions some further cases for which study has not been possible.

Norway-Sweden 1905

The events that led to an eventual peaceful outcome of the confrontation between Norway and Sweden around Norway's unilateral secession from a union with Sweden in 1905 have been documented mostly by Scandinavian researchers; there is very little to be found in English (or other European) languages. The role the workers, antimilitarist and women's movement played in them have been the focus mostly of two books: Nilsson, Torbjörn & Sørensen (eds.) 2005 and Fogelström 1971. Several details and other relevant pieces of information have been published in other books and articles, but never in the context they are presented here.

1905 The End of the Union Between Sweden and Norway

The conflicts[7] between Norway and Sweden that resulted in Norway becoming an independent state in 1905 have its roots in the Napoleonic wars. Great Britain was the main enemy of Napoleon and in 1807 Britain's preemptive attack on the Danish navy in 1807 forced Denmark, and their colony Norway, to take sides with Napoleon. Napoleon then forced Denmark-Norway

7 There were several sub-conflicts under the main issue of union versus sovereignty.

to declare war on Sweden in 1808. Due to the British naval blockade the communication between Copenhagen and Norway became extremely difficult and a provisional government was established in the Norwegian capital Christiania (now Oslo). After hundreds of years under Danish rule this first national government became the seed for a nationalistic movement in Norway. When Napoleon lost the war Norway was given to Sweden as agreed by the Treaty of Kiel in January 1814. This was not popular in Norway and resulted in a growing movement for independence.

Led by the Danish prince Christian Friedrich, Norway declared its independence. A constitutional committee presented a new Constitution based on the tripartite system of Montesquieu and with the right to vote for 40% of men above the age of 25 (Myhre, 2012:16). The new constitution was accepted on 17 May 1814.

Sweden then launched a war on Norway and soon controled most of the territory. Norway had no other choice than to accept a very unpopular union. Sweden agreed to have a separate Norwegian constitution but the king of Sweden was king of Norway as well. Foreign policy would be under Swedish control.

Most Norwegians were against having a union with Sweden. The demand for complete independence grew over time and by the end of the century the nationalist movement in Norway was a force the Swedish monarch could not ignore.

One important issue for the Norwegian Parliament from the 1880s and onwards was to establish separate consular services and eventually a separate complete foreign service for Norway. In Stockholm this was seen as a serious threat against the union and was absolutely unacceptable. In these years the views on the union divided the Swedish population, but the vast majority of the elite was strongly against "let Norway go" (Stråth, 2005:251-

397). In Norway the opposition to the union grew and the first links with friendly voices in Sweden were established.

We know that in 1893 Sweden already had made plans for "a military campaign westwards"; it was later revised and updated in 1903 (Sørensen, 2005:24).

In 1895 the Swedish king announced that, if necessary, he would use military force to keep Norway a part of the union. That changed the attitudes within Høire (the Conservative Party) in Norway. They had until then argued that Norway needed the union as a strong military defense against attacks. Sweden had at this time a much more powerful military force than Norway but Sweden decided to strengthen its capacity in order to prepare against a Norwegian show of strength. The Swedish forces had more than 200,000 soldiers in arms, Norway about 10% of that.

Norway reacted quickly and decided for massive armament. On the self-declared Day of Independence (May 17th) the Parliament agreed to buy four new coastal defense ships and twenty-two torpedo boats. The cost of the coastal defense ships alone was 19 million krones (20% of the total military budget). Old fortresses along the border were upgraded and several new ones built. Concrete plans were made for a military confrontation. Both sides prepared for war, but the asymmetric power relations stayed the same. The military budget of Norway was about 1/3 of the Swedish one in both1890 and 1905 (Berg, 2005:226).

There is no doubt that both sides prepared for a war. A report by "the History of the War Department" within the Swedish Defense Staff from 1958 documents in detail the huge efforts on both sides to be ready for war (Försvarsstaben, 1958).

The main argument for Swedish mobilization in the 1890s was not a Norwegian threat, but rather the fear of a Russian invasion. At the same time there was no lack of voices arguing for using military means to keep Norway within the union. Berg argues that with a political order to attack and to defend the armies on both sides were able, equipped and ready to start a war (Berg, 2005). A deficit of soldiers resulted in Sweden introducing obligatory conscription in 1901. But there were no guarantees that all the soldiers would follow orders. Many socialist soldiers argued that the guns should not be pointed at their brothers in Norway indicating that they saw the option of an armed uprising within the Swedish army.

Spying activities were common on either side of the border and both countries made concrete war preparations (Ottosen, 2005, Terjesen, 2001:116-138, Gäfvert, 2005, Børresen, 2004, Burch, 2005:3). The Norwegian admiral Urban Jacob Rasmus Børresen was in charge of the Norwegian fleet in Skagerak 1905 and he was in favour of a preemptive attack on the Swedish Navy (Børresen, 2005). Although he had friendly views on the union and felt loyal to King Oscar II, he did not hesitate to follow the orders Norwegian government in 1905. Børresen was a follower of the American naval ideologist Alfred Mahan and hence eager to attack the Swedish ships in open sea. Børresen came into conflict with his more reluctant and careful Commander in Chief, Admiral Sparre. When Sparre demanded that all decisions should be accepted by him, Børresen refused to leave his operative control of the fleet (Børresen, 2005). This is one more indication of how close to an open war the situation was in 1905.[8]

The Encyclopedia Britannica of 1911 states that ”war generally follows the secession of a member of a union” (Chrisholm, 1911). An indication of how tense the situation was is the fact that, when the negotiations in Karlstad took a break for four days

8 Thanks to Jacob Børresen for access to letters and other material from his ancestor's archives.

in September 1905, Sweden sent marines to the border town of Strömstad and the Norwegians responded by mobilizing troops.

The ten years from 1895 to 1905 were dominated by armaments, negotiations, provocations, public discussions, and protests. More on this will be described in the sub-chapters below.

In spring of 1905 the Norwegian parliament decided to establish their own consular institutions and when the Swedish king refused to sanction the law, the confrontation made the split a fact (Weibull, 1962). The Norwegian government resigned, but the Swedish king refused to accept their resignation. On June 7th the Norwegian Parliament declared:

"*Since all the members of the cabinet have resigned their positions; since His Majesty the King has declared his inability to obtain for the country a new government; and since the constitutional monarchy has ceased to exist, the Storting hereby authorizes the cabinet that resigned today to exercise the powers held by the King in accordance with the Constitution of Norway and relevant laws -- with the amendments necessitated by the dissolution of the union with Sweden under one King, resulting from the fact that the King no longer functions as a Norwegian King.*"[9]

Norway was de facto an independent state. But still not recognized by their former colonial power Sweden. This was not a legal decision according to international law.

The reactions in Sweden were quick and forceful. Sweden threatened with military means and the Swedish parliament demanded a referendum in Norway prior to an approval of the dissolution of the union. This shows the two main Swedish sides in this conflict: One wanted to defend the union with military means and the other could accept to allow Norway to become completely independent. Norway had discussed a referendum and were already preparing it. That the side which could accept

9 This is a translation of the main clause.

an end of the union won in the end is a direct result of the active antiwar activities in Sweden as well as in Norway. They argued that the use of war to solve the conflict was unacceptable.

The independence movement in 1814 was mainly run by an elite of powerful individuals. But in 1905 the struggle for a sovereign state was based on a broad popular nonviolent movement and democratically elected politicians in the parliament actively supporting the demand for a self-governing state. The "war-option" was never ruled out, but the opposition to use of military force was strong enough in both states to avoid such a scenario.

These are the main reasons why the conflict between Norway and Sweden 1905 is included in this study. The following chapters will explain who the main actors were, what sort or arguments they used, what they did, how their campaign was met, and the end-result.

The Antiwar movement: Secession Yes, War No

The independence movement of 1814 was carried in the first line by an elite of powerful individuals. In 1905 the struggle for an independent state was based on a broad nonviolent people movement and democratically elected politicians in parliament which actively supported the demand for self-rule. The "war option" was never excluded but the opposition in both countries was strong enough to prevent such a scenario.

These are the main reasons why the conflict between Norway and Sweden has been included in this study. The following sections will explain who the main actors have been, which arguments they used, what they did, how their campaign was seen and what the results were.

Participants in the movement including various sectors:

Workers movement

The Social Democratic parties in Sweden and Norway had their differences and conflicts, but in sum they cooperated in the struggle for Norwegian independence. The Norwegian Social Democratic party was more nationalistic than their sisters and brothers in Sweden. In Sweden the international solidarity perspective was more in the forefront of the workers movement, while the conservative parties had a stronger nationalist attitude (Hagen, 2002). In general the political parties in Sweden had different views on the union with Norway and how to react to the developing Norwegian nationalist movement.

As with most socialist parties in these years the Social Democrats were anti-militarists and in favour of international solidarity of the working class. The Swedish Social Democrats changed their view on the union in the last years of the 19th century. Leading women in the party, like Kata Dahlström, and the youth branch had for many years argued that the party should support the Norwegian demand to dissolve the union. Dahlström agitated actively that they should refuse to participate in a military attack on Norway.

Party leader Hjalmar Branting, in his speech on May 1st, 1895, said:

"*Should the horrible become a reality, and the Swedish guns ordered to march westwards, then those responsible also must consider that some who are rooted in the popular will may, without order, let fly a bullet to prevent thousands of brothers and relatives from becoming victims of military violence.*"

Everyone understood that he had the killing of Charles XII in mind. The bullet that killed him during an attack on Norway in 1718 might well have come from a Swedish gun. Branting was accused and convicted of encouraging the killing of the king and of "incitement to violence". The Supreme Court reduced his sentence from three months in prison to a fine of 300 Swedish kronor. The money was collected among workers and peace-friends in Norway and Sweden (Terjesen, 2001:185).

Led by Hjalmar Branting, the party opposed a war with Norway at their congress in 1905. When the crisis peaked Branting coined the slogan "Hands off Norway, King". Under the leadership of Branting the Social Democrats organized resistance to a call-up of reserves and threatened a general strike against a war if an attack on Norway was ordered (Store Norske Leksikon On-line). For his work in 1905 Branting shared the Nobel Peace Prize in 1921 with Christian Lange, the Norwegian secretary-general of the Inter-Parliamentary Union.

The founder of the Swedish Peace and Arbitration Society (SPAAS), a Swedish MP, and the winner of the 1908 Nobel Peace Prize, Klas Pontus Arnoldson[10] published several books and articles against war as a way to handle conflicts. Some of them were translated to Norwegian and drew a lot of attention. The poet and winner of the Nobel Prize in Literature, Bjørnstjerne Bjørnson wrote an introduction to *Law -- Not War.*[11] An English edition had an introduction from the Bishop of Durham (Magnusson, 1988:124-25). Bjørnson and Arnoldson discussed the war issue in several personal letters. Both were important public figures and voiced strong opposition to the war rhetoric. Arnoldson and SPAAS argued in favour of an international arbitration process as an alternative to the use of armies. In 1895 Arnoldson published an anonymous pamphlet with the title "Peace with Norway, even if the union crack"[12]

10 Arnoldson was radical but without a formal party affiliation in the Parliament, except in 1886 when he belonged to the Leftish Party.

11 Orgiginal publication 1887. English translation 1892.

12 In Swedish: "Fred med Norge -- Unionen må bära eller brista"

(Magnusson, 1988:147). Arnoldson was one of many voices against those who wanted to keep the union by military means.

Women against war

From 1895 onwards a growing number of women took part in the public debate about union with Norway and the resultant saber-rattling. Kata Dahlström in the Social Democratic Party was an important and early voice; many more followed. Inspired by Bertha von Suttner and her book "Die Waffen nieder" ("Down with the weapons") from 1857 the opposition to war as a way to solve conflicts received a lot of support also in the radically liberal parts of the women's movement in Scandinavia. One of the figures at the forefront was the author and celebrity Ellen Key. In 1898 she wrote a letter to her friend Anna Bugge Wicksell: "I am sick, in the innermost of my soul, of all this war rhetoric" and "We need to start building opinion for a divorce without war. We will never in eternity, I believe, agree [to war]," (Hammar, 2004:11). Key followed the public debate about the union closely and soon she took part in it herself. Her debate in newspapers with Verner von Heidenstam engaged many and influenced many more to follow the arguments.

The collapse of the union, 7 June 1905, came, as well as the threatening of war, as a surprise to most Swedes. During the following weeks Sweden was in a state of national turbulence. At least, this was how many Swedish women experienced the situation. The Conservatives condemned the Norwegian betrayal and looked with bitterness upon those Swedes taking a stand for the Norwegians. Among the Liberals there was ideological disorder since many had a hard time to overlook the way the Norwegians broke off the union. Only the socialists fully supported the Norwegians. The women found the atmosphere alarming. The most active tried to calm the warmongers through public debate. Celebrities like Ellen Key, Queen Sophia, Selma

Lagerlöf and Kata Dalström, as well as less prominent women, took positions on the conflict. The sources tell of indignation and dismay, but there are no proofs of any woman taking a stand for war against Norway. Even women who in public expressed disapproval against the breaking-up did recommend a peaceful solution. The socialist women stood unanimous behind the decision of the men to break up the union in a peaceful way. Among the Liberal women there were many working to avoid a war. There are reasons to believe that Swedish women contributed to the peaceful solution of the Swedish-Norwegian conflict in 1905. (Hammar, 2005:99)

Intellectuals

Norwegian intellectuals, authors, and artists were almost unified in favour of autonomy for Norway. Leading figures like Fritjof

Nansen and Bjørnstjerne Bjørnson (Due-Nielsen, 2005:96), as well as Gina Krogh (Blom, 2005:124-125), all argued strongly for independence. In addition to taking part in the public debate in Norway they used their international contacts to promote their views internationally. All had very good contacts with the leading Swedish figures in favour of ending the union.

Not all important groups within the Swedish and Norwegian societies had a strong consensus on the issue of union or independence. The main ones are briefly commented on below.

High ranking officers

Both the Norwegian and Swedish high ranking officers were loyal to their respective governments. If the order were given to launch a military attack they would most probably have followed such an order and used their skills to the best of their abilities. At the same time they had relatively good relations with officers from "the other" nation/state. On the Norwegian side it was the conflict between the two above mentioned marine officers, Børresen and Sparre, that could have led to an open confrontation with the Swedish marine. Børresen said: "We cannot launch a war without fighting" (Børresen and Kristiansen, 2005:106). The attitudes and actions by the hotheaded Børresen could easily have spiraled out of control (Børresen, 2005, Børresen, 2004).[13]

Another issue is to what degree they could trust their soldiers. As mentioned above the Socialist Youth and other parts of the workers movement had advanced plans for a general strike against a war and massive campaigns for refusal to follow orders among the soldiers. To what degree this threat was a serious worry for officers is difficult to know; but of course it was discussed among them. If it was seen as "a problem to handle" or they seriously feared soldiers would "turn the guns against their commanders" ... it has not been possible to confirm.

The church

The Swedish and Norwegian churches had very little contact during the years of the union (Thorkildsen, 2005:181). Every since the Reformation the Swedish church had been more conservative than their sister churches in Denmark and Norway. In general the churches played a minor role in the conflict, but their huge country-wide network played an important role in spreading and building opinions. One important exception is worth mentioning: Christopher Bruun, priest and leading figure of the Norwegian Folk-high school movement. He was a strong believer in the union as an important alliance against Russia. Only one priest was elected to Stortinget in 1903. Bishop Bang

13 In a court case after the independence both Sparre and Børresen lost their jobs due to their conflicts and behavior during the events of 1905.

in Oslo was told by a friend on June 6th that he should go to Stortinget the next day; an important announcement was to be expected. But Bang decided to go to his office as normal and get some paperwork done. Both are indication of the lack of interest for politics within the church (Thorkildsen, 2005:182-183f).

The King

King Oscar of Sweden and Crown Prince Charles John had different views on the union with Norway. Charles was more open to give Norway the independence they so obviously wanted, and Oscar wanted to keep good relations with the Norwegians within the union.

Right wing and other nationalist politicians in Sweden were all strongly against letting Norway get its independence. They saw the growing nationalist movement in Norway as a threat against the union and Sweden's right to have Norway as a part of its territory. Every step in the direction of more autonomy was seen as a weakness for the former "European super-power". The Swedish elite included few voices that supported the Norwegian demands. The exceptions were some brave women.

Part of the Swedish aristocracy, the king included, were worried about Norway becoming a republic if they got their independence. Russia, England, and Germany had the same worries (Åselius, 2005).

Sweden changed their laws to make the use of military means an option. The option of war was discussed frequently in Swedish newspapers from 1890 onwards. The Parliament doubled the "emergency war-budget" for King Oscar II and the general staff started with detailed planning of a possible war. The liberal foreign minister Carl Lewenhaupt was replaced with the ultra conservative Earl Ludvig Douglas (Stråth, 2005:349).

The conservative Swedish newspaper Vårt Land (Our Country) published an editorial December 20th 1897 expressing worries about the future of the union. Three days later an editorial had the heading: "War or Peace with Norway?" It was openly hostile and disagreed with the attitudes among Norwegians that most European states supported Norway in this conflict. The editorial argued that it was time to "tell the Norwegians that Sweden would not forever continue with the policy of concessions".

In the Swedish Parliament there were continuing proposals for economic support for the Swedish Peace and Arbitration Society (SPAAS) and their activities. They never got anything, but in 1903 a minority of 90 out of 230 MPs in the Second Chamber supported a proposal for 2500 kroners (Fogelström, 1971:91) This is a pretty good indication of the division line within the parliament.

In Norway most public voices were in favour of independence, but they did not all agreed on what means to use to achieve their independence. The preparations for a possible war got through the parliament without much opposition. The Norwegian peace movement was weaker than the Swedish one and hence had not the same influence on the national policy. The minutes from the discussion in the Norwegian Parliament of June 1905 were kept secret until 1949 but they clearly show U.S. that the war option was on the table (Stortinget 1951).

There were various strategies and forms of action:

Public discussions

Several books were published by leading representatives of the broad peace movement. Klas Pontus Arnoldson published his *Pax Mundi -- A Concise Account Of The Progress of The Movement For Peace By Means of Arbitration, Neutralization, International Law And Disarmament* in 1892 (Arnoldson, 1892). Many of those who actively opposed the war in the Swedish public discussions were editors of newspapers and other well known figures. The editors used their role to agitate against the war and promote good relations with Norway. Outside their editorial columns they frequently gave speeches at meetings. In 1895 the editor of Öresundsposten, Axel Svensson, talked to an audience of 800 in Hälsingborg. The editor of *Karlstadstidningen*, Mauritz Hellberg, talked in several meetings in Värmland. All over the country similar meetings were held (Fogelström, 1971:68-105).

Ungsocialisterna ("The Youth Socialists") with their journals *Fram* and *Brand* were antimilitarists and worked hand in hand with other parts of the workers movement for a peaceful settlement with Norway (Sørensen, 2005:26). From 1903 to 1906 *Ungsocialisterna* grew from seven clubs with around 450 members to 300-400 clubs with between 14,000 and 15,000 members. By the end of 1906 it numbered some 25,000, with a large number of local organizations (Liebknecht, 1973). At their congress in 1905 the potential war with Norway was the most discussed topic. In their publications they reacted strongly against the right wing politicians and their arguments to force Norway with military means.

Sveriges Kvinnliga Fredsförening ("The Swedish Peace Association for Women") published the journal *Ned Med Vapnen* ("Down with Armaments") and in an 1897 issue they made an appeal against the ongoing arms build-up, signed by around fifty very well respected and well known women (Fogelström, 1971:74-75).

Most of the Swedish peace movement was not, as their Norwegian sisters and brothers were, actively against the union; but they argued for respect and against the use of violence (Fogelström, 1971:76).

Swedish peace activists expanded their activities to the

international arena; relations to Norway being one main focus in addition to the relations to Russia and Finland. They worked hard to have an impact on the many conventions established to regulate international relations and warfare (Jus in Bello and Jus Ad Bellum). Their main demand was to use arbitration -- and not only when states were in conflict. The relationship to the union-partner Norway was of course central. In 1899 a group of Swedes sent a letter to Leo Tolstoy and asked him to argue for the inclusion of the conditions and terms for the conscientious objectors and the ongoing discussions at the Hague conference (Fogelström, 1971:87-88).

In summer of 1904 the fifth Nordic Peace Meeting was held in Copenhagen. They argued for including a new subject in all obligatory schools: "Peace teaching" or "Pacilogi" as it was called. The agreement on arbitration signed between Denmark and Holland was used as an example of what should be signed among all Nordic states as well. Swedish representatives were also participating at a Peace Conference in Boston, USA (Fogelström, 1971:92-93). One goal was to promote their cause internationally and collect experiences from other peace movements.

Demonstrations

SPAAS organized numerous demonstrations against war with Norway. At the May 1st 1905 demonstrations in Stockholm the branch of SPAAS there participated with around 1,000 members and a huge banner "Peace with Norway! Justice to Norway". Altogether more than 30,000 participated (Fogelström, 1971:100).

SPAAS was the host of the "Nordic Peace Meeting" in Stockholm 1895. Solidarity with brothers and sisters in other countries was the main message from that meeting. Many newspapers criticized SPAAS for being too agreeable to the Norwegian nationalists who wanted an end to the union (Fogelström, 1971:70-71).

During the years up to 1905 the peace movement had close, positive relations to the workers movement and the Social Democrats. In particular with their leader Hjalmar Branting (Fogelström, 1971:69).

Soldiers strikes and refusal to do military service

Ungsocialisterna published a text called "Down with Arms" in which they were actively promoting the idea of a general strike against war. After printing and distributing 100,000 copies the editor, Zeth Höglund, got six months in prison for mutiny. While condemned and imprisoned by the Swedish ruling class as a dangerous rebel, Höglund was saluted by others. The German socialist Karl Liebknecht described him as a hero in his book *Militarism and Anti-Militarism* (Liebknecht, 1973).

Sweden introduced conscription in 1901 and this can been seen as an important part of general armament efforts (Ericson Wolke, 2004:272, Wolke, 1999). *Ungsocialisterna* agitated against conscription and many of them were sent to prison several times for refusing to follow orders (Fernström, 1950:95-110).

The activity level was high in the two years prior to 1905. In spring 1904 the Youth Socialists printed 20,000 copies of an appeal to soldiers (Fernström, 1950:98). In May 1904 *Brand* is illustrated with the famous and strongly anti-militaristic paintings of the recently deceased Vasili Verestechagins (Fernström, 1950:100). At their congress of 1905 the Youth Socialists decided -- with a huge majority -- to expand their agitation against military conscription (Fernström, 1950:106). The clubs of Youths Socialists in Stockholm published a manifesto, "Refusal to Do

War Service". It included an appeal to collect food and other needs of the prisoners (Fernström, 1950:107).

Not all those who opposed the military refused to be soldiers. Ivar Söderholm writes in *Brand* about how they organized the Socialists Youths opposition at the Army Infantry regiment in Dalarna. They had their meetings in secret out on the shooting-range. Many of them refused to follow orders or at times they did follow orders, but slowly and with reluctance. Close to 400 joined the organization and later more than 100 were identified as "rebels" by the officers. They received relatively mild punishments (Fernström, 1950:109-110).

The Youth Socialists in Hälsingborg published and distributed 5,000 copies of a pamphlet called *Revelj* (Reveille) to soldiers (Fernström, 1950:112).

Norwegian Parliament agreed to unilaterally dissolve the union

The Norwegian Parliament, Stortinget, met on June 7th and voted unanimously in favour of unilaterally dissolving the union. The main argument was that King Oscar II did not agree to the decision to have a separate Norwegian Consular Service. This was a very provocative act and many regard these days as the peak of the conflict. Very few were informed in advance and many were taken by surprise. The state church was used as an important channel for informing the people about the decision. The following Sunday a declaration from the Parliament was read in all churches and the priests were ordered to celebrate the event with "the pure flag"[14] and nationalistic songs (Thorkildsen, 2005).

14 During the union years the official red-white-blue flag had a blue and yellow symbol in one corner to show the relation to Sweden.

The Referendum

The Swedish Parliament demanded that a referendum take place. The Norwegian Parliament then decided -- to show the unity and strength in the population -- to "ask the people". A referendum took place on August 13th 1905. All men above the age of 25 had the right to participate. Participation was 85.4 %. 371,911 votes were counted; three quarter of them from outside the cities. Of the total number of votes 3,519 were cancelled, mainly from the cities (Nielsen, 1906:442). The result was 368,208 (99.95%) in favour of dissolving the union and 184 (0.05%) against. This proved to be a very strong argument. No one could any longer doubt the will of the Norwegian people. It is one of the most lopsided referenda in history. Many Swedes saw these figures as a result of fraud; they refused to believe that the opposition to the union was that massive. No fraud was ever documented.

In 1905 only men above the age of 25 had the right to vote; but no women. Suffrage was not extended to women until 1913. Landskvindestemmeretsforeningen ("Women's National Association for the Right to Vote") wrote a letter to the Norwegian Parliament and asked to get the right to vote. Their request was turned down with the argument that they did not have the right to vote in national elections, that there were no national records of all the women in Norway, and it would be too time consuming to organize inclusion of them. Landskvindestemmeretsforeningen had at this point 2,000 members and 40 local branches. Several leading figures wanted to accept the arguments about lack of time, but members from several local groups started to collect signatures without any national coordination. Landskvindestemmeretsforeningen then decided to take the lead and organize the collection of signatures and promote and organize the referendum. The chairperson, Fredrikke Marie Qvam, was one of several who changed their minds from opposing a referendum to taking a central part in the organizing of it. This is later regarded as one of Fredrikke Marie Qvam's most important political achievements. Other famous women activists in the Association were Elise Welhaven Gunnerson and Marie Kjølseth. Altogether they collected 279,878 signatures for a peaceful dissolution of the union. This campaign later played an important role in the struggle for universal voting rights in Norway.[15]

Randhi Blehr, chair of Norsk Kvinnesaksforening (The Norwegian Association for Women's Rights), took the initiative to write a statement of support from all the women's associations in Norway. The organizing of this was taken on by the Norwegian section of the International Council of Women, led by Gina Krogh. At the day of the referendum Gina Krogh handed over to the Government statements and addresses from 565 women's associations. Prime Minister Løvland thanked the women and said: "The acts of Norwegian women from all over the country are a wonderful endowment to Norwegian history and will certainly contribute to give them the rights they demand." (Store Norske Leksikon On-line).

The government thereby had confirmation of the dissolution. 368,208 (85 percent of Norwegian men) had cast their votes, Norwegian women had collected 279,878 female signatures in favour of dissolution. The total population was 2.3 million in 1905 (Kvinneaksjon for unionsoppløsning).

---

15 Source for these facts is the database in the National Library of Norway http://www.nb.no/baser/1905/tema_folk.html accessed 2013-09-11

Repression

One obvious case of repression was imprisonment of those Swedes who refused military service and/or agitated against conscription and war with Norway. Some of these cases are mentioned in the text above. Central in this work were the Socialist Youth Organization and their local branches. In their journal *Brand* they argued strongly against war with Norway, against conscription, and in favour of a general strike against the war. The first youth who refused this service was the railway worker Josef E. Andersson from Stockholm. He was paid tribute to at the congress of 1903. Later the same year Carl August Schönqvist was arrested. He received one month in prison but was later called up again and drew two more months in prison in May 1905. Fritiof Larsson got two months hard labour plus two months in prison at a military court. Also in Skåne county *Brand* reported about more Conscientious Objectors. The organization started to collect money for financial support to the refusers and their families (Fernström, 1950:95-110). These are just a few examples. We do not have accurate and complete lists of COs from this period.

As mentioned earlier, some authors of political publications also got fines and imprisonments. Hinke Bergegren received 50 krones in fines for this public statement: "If the officers use violence against U.S., we will use the same means against them". Albert Jensen was arrested for a pamphlet published by the local branch in Norrköping. It argued strongly against accepting enrollment for military service and was printed in 68,000 copies. Jensen was also accused for a speech he gave in Mjölby. (Fernström, 1950:109).

Outcomes and Impact

The result of the referendum in Norway made it very clear what the Norwegians wanted. The Swedish Parliament had gotten a clear answer to their request. The impressive collection of signatures from the women added to the overwhelming result.

The referendum itself was of course not the only factor that played a role in this complex process in 1905. The number of statements, letters, and reports from Norwegian and Swedish authorities that year exceeds what can be covered in this chapter. For the reader who wants to study the political process in more detail I recommend "The Swedish-Norwegian union crisis: a history with documents" by Nordlund (1905). After the decision by the Norwegian Parliament to end the union with Sweden, the Swedish government resigned and an extraordinary session in the Parliament set up a commission with all parties represented to handle the final practical negotiations.

One undisputed outcome was the end of the union between Norway and Sweden. Norway become an independent and sovereign state. That was a peaceful solution to an otherwise highly armed conflict.

After the result of the referendum four delegates from each country met in the Freemason Lodge in Karlstad to negotiate the details on how to proceed. Even during the talks in Karlstad the situation was tense and both sides regarded the possibility of war as an outcome. In mid September Norway mobilized 22,500 soldiers along the border and in the navy. Sweden mobilized in the same way and placed parts of their navy in the city of Strömstad, just a few nautical miles from the border. On September 23 they reached an agreement in the negotiations in Karlstad and signed a deal. Norway had to demolish most of their fortresses and fortifications along the border and Sweden accepted a demilitarized zone on their side of the border. Both states promised to solve all future conflicts through international arbitration. The Swedish monarch Oscar II abdicated as king of Norway and Norway was soon recognized as an independent state by other states. Russia was the first one, but England and others followed soon.

Despite this agreement, almost all of the contemporary observers held that the unilateral declaration of independence and de facto separation on June 7th was not according to international law. Some Norwegians argued differently. For instance, Norwegian associate professor Nikolaus Gjelsvik argued in a 1905 article (Gjelsvik, 1905) that the Norwegian decision was a violation of the constitution but that international law had precedence over national laws and that therefore Norway acted within the legal system. His main argument was that since Sweden had threatened war against their partner in the union in1895 Norway could act as a sovereign state (Danielsen, 2005). But it is not difficult today to understand that the decision by the Parliament on June 7th was regarded by most international actors as illegal and Norway as a state had committed what could be called revolution, coup d'état, or civil disobedience.

One set of factors not discussed here are the attitudes and view of the neighbouring states and the great European states at the time of the dissolution of the union. They all followed the fall of the union closely, but had their main focus on other conflicts. Most activities were only noticed after the June 7th decision by the Norwegian Parliament. (Åselius, 2005, Jungar, 2005, Due-Nielsen, 2005). It is difficult to find valid arguments that other European states played a major role in the years leading up to the dissolution of the union.

Did "the peace movement" prevent a war? The short answer is "yes!". If we define all those diverse actors and stakeholders that each in their own way and capacities worked hard against the outbreak of a war between Norway and Sweden as a "peace movement" then there are no doubts. Without their contribution the warmongers would have won the public debate and Sweden would have used its military forces in an effort to stop the dissolution of the union with Norway. The aggressive Norwegian marine officers, with Børresen as the most extreme, would also have started a preemptive attack if it was not for the huge group of more peaceful Norwegians who argued and worked hard to prevent the use of military means.

Counterfactual history writing is an important and valuable process for anyone who wants to go deeper into the study of conflicts. The question "what would have happened if..." gives a better understanding of the situation.

Applying this to the conflicts between Sweden and Norway up until and during 1905 we find that the stakeholders, actors, and public voices arguing against the war were very important. If there would have been no one opposing the use of military means against Norway in the years prior to the secession in 1905 it is impossible to imagine that the Swedish political, military, and aristocratic leaders would not have called for a war. They had planned for years, invested enormous amounts in new weaponry, expanded their spying networks and activities, and for more than a decade argued in public that an end to the union would not be acceptable. If no voices had argued against, no activists demonstrated, no workers promoted a general strike against the war, no soldier refused participation, and no women collected signatures for a peaceful end of the conflict … what would have prevented them from doing what they wanted?

Each of the activities carried out to prevent a military confrontation can be sorted into one of the following categories: important, necessary, sufficient, counterproductive, or irrelevant. Further research is needed to judge each of the actions and campaigns and identify which category they belong to. But there is no doubt that, seen as a whole and together, they must be recognized as at least necessary for preventing the war. Were they sufficient? I have an inclination towards seeing them as sufficient, but a deeper analysis of each of the activities, as well as the context, is needed to make a well founded judgement.

The Vietnam War and the Antiwar Movement

The Vietnam war is very well documented, and also the antiwar movement against that war has been described in several studies. Before 1989 researchers only used Western sources but now also sources from Vietnam, the Soviet Union and Eastern Europe are available which show which strategic considerations played a role on the side of the opponents of the USA (Lawrence 2008:2).

A Long and Devastating War

The armed conflict in Vietnam began 1945/46 with the resistance of Vietnamese communists against France which, until 1954, had held Vietnam as a colony. In 1954 Vietnam split into a communist North, supported by the Soviet Union, and the South, considered to be part of the Western bloc. It was the time of the Cold War, with each side seeking strategic control over as many countries as possible, each fearing the other side. In the next years, a civil war developed between government troops and the insurgent Viet Cong, a communist guerilla movement which sought to unite the South with the North. In1960 the USA had 800 "advisors" in South Vietnam. By 1963 it had increased to 16,000 who supported the Southern government in its fight against the insurgency -- without the public in the USA taking much notice of the fact at that time (Davies 1989, Small 1996:115). Officially they were there for „training tasks", though later it became known that American pilots already then were flying combat missions (Small 1996:115). The increased engagement of the USA is explained mostly by internal reasons. After the Cuba crisis of 1962 President Kennedy decided that he could not afford a negative domestic reaction -- which would be encouraged by the Republicans -- if he allowed the regime in Saigon to fall into the hands of communists (Small 1996:116).

In South Vietnam, 1963 saw the first protests against Diem and against the war. Several Buddhist monks burned themselves in public and in the presence of U.S. media (which they had invited). The reports about the self-immolations contributed to Washington's support for a putsch against Diem. That putsch came after several short-term changes of government and led to a military junta with Nguyen Van Thieu and Nguyen Cao Ky taking power (Small 1996:116, Lawrence 2008:76 pp, Wikipedia).

The Vietnam war played a role during the 1964 U.S. election which was won by the Democrat Johnson. The Republican candidate Goldwater was a first-rank anti-communist who, in his book "Why not Victory"(1962), had called to throw over the communists all over the world. An important factor in Goldwater's defeat was that he had threatened in his election campaign to use nuclear bombs in Vietnam (Davies 1989:125ff, Small 1996:118).

In Vietnam meanwhile the conflict escalated though the U.S. was still trying publicly to de-emphasize their participation. In February 1965 after an incident in the Gulf of Tonkin which involved a U.S. battleship allegedly being attacked twice by North Vietnam the USA decided U.S.to start a bombing campaign against North Vietnam. Ever since July 1965 U.S. soldiers were being used as battle troops in South Vietnam (Small 1996:120). Only many years later, in 1971, did the publication of secret Pentagon papers by whistle-blower Daniel Ellsberg make it known that the incident of Tonkin Gulf did not happen the way in which the U.S. administration had claimed (Lawrence 2008:.131f). As new papers released in 2005 from the archives of NSA proved at least the second of two incidents had been invented by the National Security Agency (NSA). The incidents of 1964 had been faked by the U.S. to provide a reason to directly and openly intervene.

The war in Vietnam had two elements. In the South there was a ground war led by U.S. troops against the guerrillas of the Viet Cong (National Liberation Front). Parallel to that the U.S. bombed North Vietnam and fought against the Vietnam People's Army.

During the election in 1968, with Johnson not running for a second term, both candidates - the Democrat Humphrey and his (victorious) Republican challenger Nixon - promised to end the war. Shortly before the elections, peace talks started in Paris and there was even a break in the bombings. But the negotiations stalled quickly and the bombing was resumed (Small 1996:124, Lawrence 2008:131).

In 1969-70, under Nixon's leadership the war expanded to the neighbouring countries, Laos and Cambodia. In 1970 U.S. ground troops moved into Cambodia to destroy refuges of the Viet Cong. But the invasion was mostly unsuccessful and the troops were withdrawn the same year.

Several phases of negotiations and new offensives and bombing campaigns followed until on 27th January 1973 an agreement with North Vietnam was finally signed and the U.S. withdrew its ground troops. The bombing of Cambodia continued for a while however, until the Watergate Scandal put an end to them. That scandal, caused by a break-in into the HQ of the Democratic Party triggered a number of further illegal acts of the administration and made the Congress force President Nixon to end all military operations in Indochina by the middle of August 1973 (Lawrence 2008:164 pp). That same year the U.S. abolished conscription (Brock & Young 1999: 263 pp).

The war that had cost altogether the lives of three million people ended in 1975 with the occupation of the South Vietnamese capital Saigon (today Ho Chi Minh City) and the reunification of Vietnam. In Cambodia in 1975 the Khmer Rouge under Pol Pot came to power and killed about two million Cambodians until they were removed by a Vietnamese military intervention in 1979.

The Antiwar Movement: Stop the War in Vietnam

The movement against the Vietnam war is probably one of the best researched cases of an antiwar movement. Also in publications in political science about the war and international politics the movement is mentioned though the assessment of its influence varies. At first glance surprising is that the role of the movement in ending the war is emphasized by some of the "hawks" who created a stab-in-the-back legend ('the war against communism was lost at home'). While some of those close to the movement are much more sceptical about its outcomes.

The movement was initiated by 'old', pre-existing peace organisations (see section 2.2.3 below). It gained participants through a combination of several factors, the media reports on the war undoubtedly being of them. Another was the inclusion of students in the military draft – earlier they mostly had been exempted.

The movement stood in interaction with the civil rights movement of the blacks in the U.S. and with a cultural change that, starting in the U.S., quickly reached Europe and other industrial countries. It was carried by the (mostly white) hippie movement of the earlier 1960s and the student movement at the end of the 1960s. The hippie movement rejected the structures of authority of the old society, including its sexual morals and its music. The musical "Hair" established itself (and the war in Vietnam) as an exemplary monument.[16] The students' movement began in France in 1968 and spread from there quickly to all other West European countries and to the U.S. where it intermingled with the antiwar movement where students already played a role before 1968 (s. Carter 1992:86 pp). It was mostly characterized by politically left analyses and positions.

At the beginning of the 1960s the engagement of the USA in Indochina found little public interest and the government knew that the population was on its side in the fight against communist regimes. The first public protests happened in 1963, organised by the War Resisters' League, the U.S. section of the War Resisters' International, an antimilitarist-pacifist umbrella founded after World War One.

In 1965 the first large demonstrations happened. The first antiwar demonstration in Washington organised by the Students for a Democratic Society (SDS) saw 20,000 participants in April 1965 (Isserman 1992).

In the following years the protest grew and opinion polls showed that the rejection of the war, earlier the position of a tiny minority, grew in the American public. The war, though, still found the agreement of the majority of U.S. citizens at least until 1970/71.

The peak of the antiwar movement was in 1967-68. In April 1967 100,000 people demonstrated in Washington against the war, and the demand to withdraw the troops grew very loud

16 Many activists of the organised peace movement were critical to the 'counter culture' (see Farber 1992).

in the face of TV reports on the cruelty of the war. [17] Also in 1967 Martin Luther King took a position against the war (Wells 1994:117ff).

In October 1969 altogether more than three million people participated in antiwar protests in more than 200 cities. The main demand was a moratorium (McReynolds 1992). In November 1969 500,000 people demonstrated in Washington (Cortright 2008:162).

In 1970 there were violent student protests and a country-wide strike of students, with an estimated participation of eight million, triggered by the death of four students killed by the National Guard during protests at the Kent State College.

When Nixon announced the end of the ground war in Cambodia and the numbers of the U.S. troops were more and more reduced from 1970 on, the antiwar movement also lost its impetus, though protests continued through 1971 and 1972 (Wells 1994:449). In 1971 only 15,000 people participated in a demonstration in Washington (McReynolds 1992).

An important element of the antiwar movement was war resistance by draftees and soldiers -- young men refusing to be drafted or evading the draft by fleeing to third countries; and soldiers and veterans joining the war protests.[18] The war became so unpopular with the soldiers that there was extremely bad morale in the troops from c. 1969 on. Drugs were a major problem and there were numerous cases of open refusal

17 For example, reports on the My Lai massacre were first presented as a ‚regrettable single case'. But it soon became clear that it was not such an isolated individual case (Meyrowitz & Campbell 1992:130 pp)

18 For example 2,000 Vietnam veterans organized in April 1971 a four-day „invasion" of Washington during which, in torn uniforms, they threw their medals on the steps of the Capitol (Lawrence 2008:151).

to obey orders and even the killing of officers, the so-called “fragging”(Jeffreys-Jones 1999:118f, Lawrence 2008:151).[19]

The typical member of the antiwar movement was a younger white man from the middle class. Women were also engaged but often found themselves in subordinate roles (Echols 1992:173). Swerdlow (1992:159) reports that in one case women were refused the right to speak in a public event because they were deemed, as non-combatants, not to be involved. [20]

Most soldiers in contrast, at least two thirds of them, belonged to the lower classes, and many of them were black (Cortright 2008:184). Their resistance against the war -- that they initially had supported – also grew (see below). Also beginning in 1967 Martin Luther King, as the leader of the moderate wing of the civil rights movement, spoke out against the war.. But there was undoubtedly a (cultural and class) gap between the resisting soldiers and the bourgeois protest movement that could not be overcome.

The trade unions mostly supported the war though in 1969 some of them split from the main umbrella organisation (the AFL-CIO) and joined the ranks of the antiwar movement (Benedict 1977:80, Cortright 2008:179).

19 Derived from the term „fragmentation grenades“ that were thrown into the tents of officers. In the literature there is different information on the frequency of such incidents. According to Anderson, in 1970 alone soldiers refused about 30 orders to attack („combat refusal“), and until December 1972 between 800 and 1,000 cases of (attempted) killing of officers and more than 1,400 deaths for unknown reasons were counted (Anderson 1992:105). Cortright gives the number of 551 for such incidents between 1969 and 1972 … with 86 dead and 700 injured officers (Cortright 1992:123).

20 This has also served as a catalyst for the emerging feminist movement – many women started to organise themselves in womens‘ groups and to analyse patriarchical structures of oppression (Overy 1982:36).

The antiwar movement consisted of a number of organisations. The most important were probably:

- Students for a Democratic Society (SDS), a leftist group whose leadership leaned towards Maoism. The SDS had in 1966 less than 15,000 members; some years later c. 100,000 (Isserman 1992:23)
- War Resisters' League, an old pacifist-antimilitarist organisation with socialists, anarchists and other antimilitarists among its ranks.
- The co-called "old left" with Trotskyists from various groups, for example the Socialist Workers' Party (SWP). They focussed on legal protests only as an instrument (Cortright 2008:157pp). Their main slogan, coined in 1965, was: „Bring the boys home now"(Brock & Young 1999: 263pp).
- SANE, an organisation that was founded in the 1950s against nuclear weapons. They always combined protest and advocacy work and did so also as part of the antiwar movement (Cortright 2008:157 pp).
- Clergy and Laymen Concerned About Vietnam – CALCAV was an interreligious group of Christians and Jews21 founded in 1963 because of consternation caused by the self-immolation of Buddhists in Vietnam.
- Other important groups in the movement were, among others, the U.S. branch of the Fellowship of Reconciliation, the Ecumenical Interreligious Committee on Vietnam, the National Council for Churches, the Catholic Peace Fellowship, the Union of Marican Hebrew Congregations, the American

21 It is not clear if there were also Buddhists and / or Muslims among their members.

Friends Service Committee and the Catholic Worker Movement (Hall 1992).

- The Committee for Nonviolent Action (CNVA) specialized in actions of civil disobedience.
- Vietnam veterans formed one of the most important organisations of the time, the Vietnam Veterans against the War. They counted in 1971 20,000 members. Among them 2,000 active soldiers still in Vietnam (Cortright 2008:166).

In 1965 most of these groups formed a coalition against the Vietnam war. The coalition suffered however from different positions towards North Vietnam. Some groups took the side of the North, while others rejected the war of both sides (Brock & Young 1999: 278 pp).

A sector of its own was the movement around conscientious objection and GIs. It was not a unified movement but was characterized by many individual decisions of the recruits and soldiers concerned (see Anderson 1992, Chatfield 1990:388 pp). First, there were the young men[22] who escaped the draft by fleeing to other countries (Canada, Europe or Australia), or who stayed and declared themselves war resisters which often led to prison sentences. (The first three COs in 1966 had to serve three years in prison.) The public burning of draft papers that became a type of action from 1967 on has remained unforgotten until this day. Altogether about 570,000 young men became classified as „draft offenders". 8,750 were sentenced and c. 3,250 had to serve a prison sentence (Cortright 2008:165). 170,000 men were classified as COs (Cortright 2008:167).

Second, there were those who resisted the war while being in the military. There were various underground magazines. War

22 Women were not drafted and their possibilities to join voluntarily was much limited at that time.

resisters met with people who thought like them and with civil supporters in so-called antiwar cafés established in close vicinity to military bases. Active GIs publicly criticized the war: for example there was a full-page advert in 1969 in the New York Times, signed by 1,366 active soldiers (Cortright 2008: 165).

Especially in the last years of the war the number of deserters increased dramatically, including more and more volunteers, not only those being drafted (McReynolds 1992:63). And last but not least there was a lot of passive and sometimes also active and violent resistance of the soldiers in Vietnam itself (see above). On the whole it is estimated that every fourth soldier in one or the other form joined protests against the war (Cortright 2008:165).

The antiwar movement was characterized by different positions in several regards. One dividing line was between those who, coming from the political left, sided in the war with the cause of North Vietnam. They were however a minority. The majority were either pacifists rejecting all wars (like WRL) or people who were very sceptical about socialisms of any type, be it the Soviet or the Chinese variant, but who considered war not an appropriate means to fight it.

Part of the activists were recruited from those opposing certain types of weapons (e.g. nuclear weapons) or because they had a problem with certain acts of the U.S. military in that war that was seen as a "dirty war" (bombing of Hanoi, mining of Haiphon, napalm, deforestation, antipersonnel weapons, threat of tactical nuclear weapons, atrocities against civilians (Overy 1982, DeBenedetti 1990: 88ff).

These different motivations led to three positions regarding the ending of the war:

1. Favouring an unconditional military victory of North Vietnam;

2. "Stop the killing now"– the call for a cease-fire that implied an agreement of the warring parties or a unilateral ending of the military engagement of the U.S.

3. Unilateral withdrawal of the U.S. troops even if that meant that the communists won (Brock & Young 1999:280f).

The two main faces of the antiwar movement were the mass demonstrations in Washington and other cities and the resistance of draftees and soldiers that included many elements of civil disobedience, for example the burning of draft cards. The main strategy of the movement was to move the administration and the U.S. president to change its policies. In times of presidential elections, many activists hoped that a candidate would be elected who would meet the demand to end the war. In spite of that there seems to have been no real dialogue between the antiwar movement and the top level of the administration. The communication mostly happened mediated through media (Wells 1994:1).

The main exception to this seems to have been some lobbying of the Congress with the goal to win over members of the Congress in the hope that they then would resist the president's pro-war decisions (Dumbrell 1989b:107pp, among others by the Friends Committee on National Legislation (David Grant, personal communication)..

The antiwar movement had a problem in gaining the support of the majority of the population. On the contrary, in opinion polls of the 1960s a high percentage of U.S. Americans found the anti-war movement "disgusting". During most of the war the majority was in favour of the it, not against it. Only in 1970/71 did this change (Garfinkel 1997:17, Cortright 2008:164).[23]

23 By the end of 1967, 45 % of Americans believed that the military intervention in Vietnam had been a mistake (Lawrence 2008:111 pp). In 1965 still 57% had supported the politics of the U.S. in Vietnam;

However there seems to be no causal relationship between the rejection of the movement and the support for the war. There were other, third, reasons -- like patriotism – that determined attitudes (Garfinkel 1997:17). That means that people did not support the war because they hated the antiwar movement but because they saw themselves as patriots supporting their government. But there was obviously a connection to the voting behaviour of the Americans. Garfinkel, at least, explains the victory of Richard Nixon as a backlash against the antiwar movement (1997:163).

Protests against the war did not only take place in the USA. There were also protests in many European countries and in Canada. In addition there were protests in South Vietnam itself, especially by Buddhist monks. But these international aspects seem not to have found much attention in the USA itself (Brock & Young 1999:281). At least they did not play a role in the strategies of the antiwar movement. One reason may have been that in Europe it was the students' movement that dominated the protests. And the (European) students declared themselves to be in solidarity with the opponents of "U.S. imperialism" (Benedict 1977:99).

Repression

The U.S. severely persecuted war resisters and deserters – they usually were sentenced to prison. In demonstrations police mostly only intervened if violent protest threatened. In 1970 however, the National Guard shot four students at Kent State College which led to massive, violent student protests and a nation-wide student strike of eight million.

---

only 24% thought it was a mistake and one third thought that the demonstrators had no right to protest (Wells 1994:63). By 1971 a majority of 58% thought that it had been „morally wrong" to fight in Vietnam (Lawrence 2008:151).

Furthermore, the movement was object of massive intelligence efforts by the CIA. At the end of 1967 President Johnson asked the CIA to start an illegal surveillance programme directed at the leaders of the protest. With the name "Operation Chaos" this programme collected information over the next seven years on 300,000 Americans (Lawrence 2008:119) with the objective to discredit the protest leaders (Carter 1992:99 pp). At the beginning of the 1970s the Nixon administration then tried to move against the movement in a concerted action to suppress it through massive police actions at demonstration. During the four days of the "March on Washington" in 1971 13,400 people were arrested.

Outcomes and Impact

The participation of U.S. ground troops in the Vietnam war lasted eight years. The troops were withdrawn after a settlement that reflected the victory of North Vietnam. What was the contribution of the antiwar movement to this end? And secondly, have there been decisions during the course of the war that can be attributed to influence by the movement?

To begin with the second question: There can be little doubt that the protests influenced political decisions of the U.S. government during the war.

- Overy writes that the U.S. decided not to use nuclear bombs due to the protests (Overy 1982: 38).24
- About President Johnson in particular it is reported that he was personally conflicted and that he felt to be under extreme external pressures, including by his friends and advisors (Wells 1994:106ff, Small 1984:8f). That he did not run for a second term of office and

24 Overy is however the only source for this that the author could find..

proposed negotiations to end the war may have been a direct consequence (Lawrence 2008:129f, 137; Small 1996:121ff). However the movement was not strong enough to achieve the election of a candidate who would realize its objectives. Richard Nixon followed Johnson in the office -- i.e., a president who escalated the war further, probably also because the protests on the streets made people afraid of disorder (McReynolds 1992:70).

- In the reign of Johnson, the question was whether an invasion of North Vietnam should be attempted. Johnson decided against it because he doubted the effectiveness and feared an intervention by China. But also because he feared the reaction at home (Wells1994:154p).
- After the Tet Offensive (30 January-23 February1968) by North Vietnam and the Vietcong the U.S. deliberated whether more troops should be sent. President Johnson eventually decided against it, allegedly less due to the protests on the street, but more because a panel of independent foreign policy advisers dissuaded him. "Far more than protests on campuses or in the streets, the defection of these powerful men – all of them from the business, legal, and policy-making elite – convinced Johnson that he had to do something dramatic" (Lawrence 2008:129) This can also be interpreted as an example of how the division of elites can bring about bring political change.
- 1969 Nixon began to escalate the war and to bomb Cambodia (Small 1996:124 pp). In October of that year, at the same time Nixon was presenting a secret ultimatum to rebel leader Ho Chi Minh, there were

mass demonstrations of over three million – without the protesters knowing of the ultimatum. „Nixon had to take them into account when he permitted the November 1 deadline to pass without any action."(Small 1996:125). Nixon allowed the ultimatum to pass without taking action.

- During Nixon's term the movement prevented a larger escalation of violence. Nixon himself admitted influence of the movement to his decisions, but said it was the peace movement's fault that his efforts to end the war in 1969 were not successful (Cortright 2008:161 pp).

As for the ending of the war, there are, as noted in the introduction, different points of view concerning the role of the movement.

Many authors as well as political and military actors of that time think that the antiwar movement had a significant impact on the warfare of the U.S. and made it responsible for the withdrawal of the United States. This includes not only opponents of the war, but also pro-war protagonists who blame antiwar movement for the defeat of the United States. Some generals even spoke of a "stab in the back". General Schwarzkopf (1992) is quoted: „*We were fighting with one hand tied behind our back*" (Cortright 2008:163).

As several authors claim, the movement had made the war unpopular, had contributed to a lack of personnel in the military, had caused a split within the elites and had led to morale collapse in the military itself (Overy 1982: 38, Dumbrell 1989a:1f, Cortright 2008:157, Carter 1992:97ff). According to Jeffrey-Jones, the reasons for the success of the antiwar movement were that, for the White House, the protests were unexpected and surprising. And that the disorganization and disunity of the movement itself contributed to the confusion of the government because it made the movement unpredictable. Also the sequence of protests with different aspects -- first of students, then of blacks, then of women had -- a cumulative effect (Jeffreys -Jones 1999: 3).

„*It is said by supporters of the Vietnam War that the war was lost not in Vietnam but in the antiwar movement in America. I hope that is a correct analysis. It would be the highest tribute both to the antiwar movement and to American democracy if it could be firmly established that organized public opinion and political action were responsible for correcting the enormous blunders of the leaders who took U.S. into the jungles of Vietnam.*"(McGovern 1992:xii)

But beside the antiwar movement's influence, as President Jimmy Carter (1992:97 pp) pointed out, there were other factors that made a great impact on the war. While the war in the South alone was not winnable, the fear of a Soviet or Chinese intervention -- which may have been triggered by an invasion of North Vietnam or the use of nuclear weapons -- was a significant factor. This was in addition to the pressure on the U.S. administration that the movement had built up over the years.

The secondary literature used for this study here does not yield sufficient information regarding the question of the attitude of the protesters regarding their opponents. In the introduction it was outlined that according to the theory proposed by Martin Arnold, the conscious attempt to win the opponents over, not to meet them as enemies to be defeated, was a crucial element of success in the view of the three nonviolent protagonists[25] he researched. It seems that such attempts were made regarding the soldiers sent to Vietnam, but little in regard to those who sent them. As previously mentioned, it was quoted that communications mostly happened through the media rather than directly.

25 Mohandas K. Gandhi, Hildegard Goss-Mayr and Bart de Ligt.

As to the impact of the movement, in the literature there is also a contrary view to be found. This refers essentially to three points: 1.) that, at least in the first years, the antiwar movement was rejected by the majority of the population; 2.) that the presidents were afraid to give in to "the street ", and thereby the movement hampered a peace agreement with North Vietnam; and 3.) that North Vietnam took the antiwar movement into its calculations, which also prevented an early end to the war.

Regarding #1: The movement was for a very long time unable to get the majority of the population on its side, leading regularly in elections to a backlash against the movement. Berkowitz (1973) [26] investigated, based on Gallup polls, whether or not there was a correlation between demonstrations and the opinion of the population regarding the war. He found that the only connection -- from the point of view of the protesters – was a negative one. After large demonstrations the numbers of those approving the action of the president increased slightly. The long-term drop in support for the war could of course still have had something to do with the movement. But Berkowitz suggests that there are more plausible theories to explain this: e.g. a direct correlation with the number of U.S. soldiers killed, a factor that had already shown a direct correlation (Schreiber 1976: 227) [27] in the Korean War.

According to Dumbrell quantitative studies tend "*to portray antiwar activities as having a negligible or ambivalent effect in turning either elite or public opinion against the war*"(Dumbrell 1989a 3). In fact, the figures show that even in 1971, when the majority of the population finally did not want the war, considerable numbers still rejected the antiwar movement (Cortright 2008:163, Garfinkle 1997:17)[28]

26 Schreiber 1976.

27 His source is John E. Mueller (1973) War, Presidents and Public Opinion. New York: Wiley, p. 70.

28 Even in mid 1970s the SDS (Students for Democratic Society)

Regarding #2: According to some authors, the concern of the rulers to be perceived as weak -- when they gave in to the demands of the movement -- led to the fact that the demonstrations intensified the support of the silent majority for the war ... and therefore ultimately contributed to the prolongation of the war (Garfinkle 1997:13: 163f). „*The antics of the radical antiwar movement deterred more Americans from opposing the war sooner because they were afraid of the company they would have to keep by so doing.*" (Garfinkle 1997: 13)[29]

Regarding #3: Johnson and Nixon both often claimed that the antiwar movement prolonged the war because it strengthened Hanoi's belief that a withdrawal of the U.S. troops might be enforced by the street protests. North Vietnam would have otherwise yielded more or earlier in the negotiations (Small 1984:2). In fact, they may have been right. As was documented after the opening of the archives, the warring parties in Vietnam included the protests in the United States in their calculations. Lawrence writes that North Vietnam was not only convinced of its military victory, but also of the fact that growing public opposition to the war in the U.S. would eventually force the U.S. to make peace on the terms of North Vietnam (Lawrence 2008:13 / 141; Jeffrey Jones 1999:3). In 1969 North Vietnam refused therefore U.S. offers to withdraw troops on both sides.[30]

The conclusion that can be drawn from these partially conflicting observations is threefold:

1. The antiwar movement took place in a time of cultural change,

---

was named as a „highly unfavourable"group by 42%, ranking higher than the John Birch Society and the Black Panthers (Garfinkle 1997: 18).

29 He quotes: John P. Robinson, "Balance Theory and Vietnam-Related Attitudes", Social Science Quarterly 53,1, December 1970.

30 Also Overy mentions the antiwar movement strengthening the morale of North Vietnam (Overy 1982: 38).

was influenced by it, and shaped it. The hippie movement, the student movement, the U.S. civil rights movement and the women's movement changed the political and social culture, not only in North America but throughout the global North. The negative opinion polls in the U.S. are, therefore, hardly surprising.

2. Between the presidential elections the movement succeeded to influence the conduct of the war by the U.S. government, occasionally to prevent escalation of the war and to exert influence on the elites. But its strength was not enough to force rapid peace making. And every election then there was a backlash, because the majority of the population preferred presidential candidates who were aggressive towards the war.

3. The end of the war was primarily a military defeat -- but a defeat that was at least partly caused by the apparently disastrous conditions within the U.S. military. And this fact, the reluctance of a large number of soldiers to wage war in Vietnam, had much to do with the success of the antiwar movement.

As with other peace movements there were clearly a number of other effects that are not directly related to the goal of ending the war. So Wasmuth points to the creation of organizations "*that still are relevant today for the peace work during the '80s*" (Wasmuth 1987:94, translation CS). Subsequent antiwar movements have repeatedly referred to the Vietnam War and the movement against it. And the warning of a "second Vietnam" has, to date, significant weight in public debates. Another consequence of the movement and the two government scandals that were related to it (Pentagon Papers and Watergate) was that generally the trust in the government was badly damaged, such as opinion polls in the first half of the 1970s show (Dumbrell 1989b: 101).

The Movement Against the Contra War of the 1980s in Nicaragua

The movement against the U.S. support to the so-called Contras in Nicaragua in the 1980s is less well documented than the antiwar movement against the Vietnam war. The main sources for this chapter have been a study published by Roger Peace in 2012 and the writings of Griffin-Nolan on the organisation Witness for Peace.

Nicaragua: Right-wing Discontent Is Instrumentalized By the United States

After a 2-year armed uprising the leftist FSLN (Sandinistas) toppled dictator Somoza and came to power in July 1979. The civil war had cost the lives of 50,000 people (Peace 2012:12). While the Democratic U.S. President Carter grudgingly accepted the change of power in Nicaragua, his Republican successor Reagan, elected in 1980, started to take steps against what he called the "Marxism in Latin America".

After the victory of the Sandinistas, members of the Somoza regime's National Guard formed a guerrilla insurgency. They were supported by Argentine Special Forces and by the CIA. Between 1982 and 1990 the "Contras" engaged in a bloody civil war with the aim of removing the Sandinistas. Their main instrument was terror against the civil population. The Contras were supported right from the beginning by the USA.

In 1983 the House and Senate fought about the financing of the Contras, with the Democrat-dominated House against it and the Republican-dominated Senate for it. Beginning then in 1984 funds flowed to the Contras (Peace 2012:81). The funds were temporarily stopped later in 1984 when the mining of Nicaraguan ports in a CIA operation caused outrage in the Congress.

However, shortly afterwards it granted "non-lethal" aid to the Contras, and from 1986 official military aid flowed again (Peace 1988:220), in spite of a ruling of the International Court of Justice (ICJ). The ICJ ruled in favor of Nicaragua and against the United States and awarded reparations to Nicaragua. The ICJ held that the U.S. had violated international law by supporting the Contras in their rebellion against the Nicaraguan government and by mining Nicaragua's harbors. The United States refused to participate in the proceedings after the Court rejected its argument that the ICJ lacked jurisdiction to hear the case. The U.S. later blocked enforcement of the judgment by the United Nations Security Council and thereby prevented Nicaragua from obtaining any actual compensation.

In 1987 a new scandal rocked politics in America, the so-called Iran-Contra affair. It became known that the administration had sought funds to support the Contras by selling arms to Iran (Peace 2012:208). Thenceforward the Congress approved once more only "non-lethal aid". In1989 George Bush Sr. took over from Ronald Reagan and changed the strategy of his predecessor. Bush focused on influencing the elections in Nicaragua in 1990. The Sandinistas lost those elections and the United States ended the war.

The Contras operated mainly from bases in Honduras and Costa Rica. In the fall of 1984, a CIA manual became public which described techniques of the terrorist attacks (Peace 2012:178). The CIA trained the Contras and was responsible for military operations of its own. The CIA blew up oil tankers and, as mentioned, in 1984 the CIA mined the port of the capital. In the same year, the U.S. conducted a large-scale, six-month military manoeuvre ("Big Pine II") in Honduras, where 5,000 U.S.

soldiers were involved. It has been suggested by many observers that this was a preparation for a direct military intervention, an invasion of Nicaragua, and, indeed, it has become known since then that there was a plan to entice the Nicaraguan military to pursue the rebels into Honduras which would have provided a pretext for the invasion (Peace 2012:22 pp).

The victims of the Contra war: 30,000 dead, 350,000 displaced persons, 9 billion USD damage (Peace 2012:24).

The Antiwar Movement: No Support to the Contras in Nicaragua

The movement against the Contra war took place over the entire period of the conflict from 1982 to 1990. Also after that many groups continued to pursue the events in Nicaragua and other Latin American countries. The movement consisted of initiatives and church groups that came from solidarity work with Latin America that had already been active at the time of uprising of the Sandinistas. The movement also contained some groups which had been active in the Vietnam War (Peace 2012:53). The protests against the war could not numerically compare at any time with those of the anti-Vietnam war movement. The movement was characterized primarily by the fact that it linked decentralized protests and public relations activities (besides occasional nonviolent direct action) with delegations and longer-term presence of volunteers to Nicaragua). The movement coincided with the anti-nuclear peace movement which campaigned against the deployment of new medium-range nuclear missiles in Europe (see 2.4). In Europe there was a close connection between the two movements.

Peace (2012:63 pp) lists several groups that have been part of the movement:

- Progressive religious networks, many of whom had also been active in the days of the Vietnam War (Jesuits, the Quaker AFSC, Fellowship of Reconciliation, Clergy and Laity Concerned)
- Leftist groups
- Human rights activists
- Scientists who had to do with Latin America
- Non-religious anti-Vietnam war groups (SANE, Vietnam Veterans Against War, War Resisters' League, WILPF).

Together there may have been about 1,000 local groups in the movement (Peace 2012:212).

As in the case of the Vietnam War there were differences between the antiwar groups in regard to the position to the regime against which the war was directed. Many of the groups were sympathetic to the Sandinistas but not all. But unlike the Vietnam antiwar movement there was agreement in the central demands:

- Immediate end to the support of the Contras;
- No invasion of Nicaragua by the United States;
- After 1985: the end of the embargo (Peace 2012:46, 63 pp).

The main arguments of the movement were (Peace 2012:37 pp):

- The support of the Contras was a violation of international law (sovereignty of states, no right to intervention);
- You must have learned from the Vietnam war;
- Diplomacy instead of war ;

- Criticism of terrorism (especially after the aforementioned CIA manual, a guide for terrorism, became known).
- The issue of violation of laws of the United States played a smaller role (e.g., against the mining of the harbours of Nicaragua). This was perhaps because many of the activists had an ambivalent relationship to the legal system itself, coming from a tradition of civil disobedience.

The movement began about 1982, concurrent to the escalation of the war in Nicaragua.

In 1983 members of different church congregations from the United States visited Nicaragua and were emotionally moved when they saw a place where there had just been a Contra raid. The impressions of this journey led to the founding of the organization Witness for Peace that, from 1983 on, organised regular two-week delegations and long-term teams to Nicaragua (Griffin-Nolan 1991 and 2000). At the same time, supported by the Nicaragua Solidarity movement[31], a movement emerged of international brigades which came into the country for work assignments – for example, helping with the sugar cane harvest. Overall, it is estimated that more than 20,000 people went as members of international brigades to Nicaragua (Peace 2012:171). The objectives of these delegations and presence were two-fold. First, it was preventing violence by the presence of the activists and it was raising the price for a possible U.S. intervention (Griffin -- Nolan 2000:302). Second,, and at least as important, the reports of the returnees were an essential element of public relations in the United States. The work had as an objective to bring the reality of the war closer to the people of the United States. For this purpose, once a year a "Central

31 In Germany it was a centre in Wuppertal that organized such deployments.

America Week" and a media campaign were organized (Peace 2012:96). Witness for Peace was just one of the organizations that organized such delegations. A large part of visiting travel was handled by two professional tour operators. For example, around the time of the elections in Nicaragua in October 1984 one operator organized 24 tours of 10 to 14 days each (Peace 2012:102 pp).

The presence in Nicaragua by Witness for Peace and the international brigades involved a considerable risk. According to Peace (2012:171) 14 volunteers lost their lives, four were raped and 59 temporarily kidnapped. [32]

A first large central demonstration took place on 12 November 1983 in Washington, shortly after the U.S. invasion of Grenada, in which 20,000 people participated (Peace 2012:87). At a demonstration in 1985 according to the organizers up to 100,000 people took part, although the police estimated only 26,000 (Peace 2012:181). In October 1986 in response to the approval of new aid to the Contras by the Congress, demonstrations took place in at least 15 cities (Peace 2012:193). 1987 saw seven weeks of actions at the Capitol, organized by religious groups such as Witness for Peace, which became known under the name "The Mobe". These protests were combined with actions of civil disobedience, inter alia, at the headquarters of the CIA (Peace 208:208 pp).

In the fall of 1984, when the possibility of a direct military intervention (i.e., invasion) of the United States was becoming more realistic, a number of groups published a declaration of commitment (Pledge of Resistance). It ended with the sentence: *"If the armies of the United States are mobilized to wage war on Nicaragua, may a mighty nonviolent army of U.S. citizens also be mobilized to wage peace"*(Peace 2012:88).

32 See also the website of WfP; Howard 2001 und Griffin-Nolan 2000.

The declaration was subsequently to become an important mobilization tool. In 1985, already 55,000 people had signed it. In 1987 there were around 100,000 signatures (Peace 2012: 208).

Also in 1985 large actions of civil disobedience were held with around 10,000 people in total participating. This included, for example, the occupation of the offices of a U.S. Senator and penetration into the John F. Kennedy Federal Building (Peace 2012:183). In September-October 1986, a fast of four Vietnam veterans drew public attention (Peace 2012:192).

Another instrument of the movement was lobbying, especially in Congress, with the aim that the financial aid for the Contras would be stopped. This lobbying was conducted mainly by the group Coalition For New Foreign and Military Policy (CNFMP). In 1988 prominent religious leaders signed a statement against aid to the Contras (Peace 2012:90 pp).

The movement was also supported by initiatives from other countries, both in Latin America and Europe. In many countries, groups formed and sent volunteers in so-called solidarity brigades to Nicaragua. In July 1984, Norwegian activists organized a solidarity ship loaded with medicine, school materials, fertilizer and newsprint rolls. Four Nobel Laureates -- Adolfo Perez Esquivel, Betty Williams, George Wald and Linus C. Pauling - participated in the trip (Peace 1212:82).

Repression

The reaction of the U.S. government to the movement was primarily to denigrate the groups involved as Marxist and pro-Soviet Union. To this end, they also paid right-wing think tanks (Peace 2012:146 pp).

Outcomes and Impact

As in the case of the Vietnam antiwar movement influence on the warfare must be distinguished from impact on the ending of the war. Analysts of the movement name two main impacts:

1. The movement had influence in stopping the financial aid for the Contras. But it was by no means the movement alone but also diplomatic efforts of Latin American countries and the fact that one of the two major parties in the U.S., the Democrats held skeptical views on the war and, when they had the majority in both houses,took advantage of the opportunity to stop or diminish funding (Small 1994:3-4). At the same time the crossing of the border to Honduras by Nicaraguan troops, which a few years earlier might have been seen as a reason for direct military intervention, did nothing to change the fact that the military assistance remained stopped (Peace 2012:223). Contrary to public perception, however, the war was not yet over; but in the middle of the 1989 presidential election (won by George H. W. Bush) it was difficult for the campaign to spread this message (Peace 2012:235).

2. With some plausibility it can be argued that the decision of the United States not to resort to a direct invasion can be attributed to the antiwar movement. Oliver North, the man responsible for the Iran-Contra deal, lamented that the first barrier to overcome, in deciding upon an invasion, was the domestic opposition (Peace 2012:4-5).

The Anti-Nuclear Peace Movement of the 1980s in Germany

The peace movement of the 1980s is the object of several studies of movement researchers from different countries. [33] This chapter focuses on the West German peace movement which allowed the author to refer to -- besides the various studies -- her own memories, personal correspondence and grey literature (ephemeral materials)[34].

Nuclear Middle-Range Missiles: Arming to Disarm?

In 1979 NATO announced that it would respond to the stationing of Soviet intermediate-range nuclear SS-20 missiles with the deployment of its own medium-range missiles in Europe if the Soviet Union did not agree to a disarmament of the SS-20. This decision was made in the time of U.S. President Carter who had previously been pursuing the goal of developing a neutron bomb -- a plan which he dropped after massive protests. His successor Ronald Reagan escalated anti-Soviet rhetoric, pursued a policy of "peace through strength", wanted to exhaust the Soviet Union by the arms' race, and speculated about a nuclear war in Europe (Peterson 2011:8). With the name "dual-track decision" or "retrofit decision", NATO thereby instigated a peace movement in Western Europe unprecedented in size and diversity. Also in the USA there was a numerically strong movement for the freezing of nuclear

33 E.g. Wasmuht 1987, Risse-Kappen 1988, Leif 1990, Meyer 1999, Wittner 2007, Cortright 2008, Goers w.d.., Aufsätze in Marullo & Lofland 1990.

34 For example the website of the Friedenskooperative (www.friedenskooperative.de/netzwerk/histo000.htm).

armaments ("The Freeze Movement"). But the movement was not able to prevent NATO's deployment of the Pershing II and Cruise Missiles from 1982/83 onward. NATO stationed 108 Pershing II missiles in the Federal Republic of Germany (among other places in Mutlangen) and 464 cruise missiles in Europe -- Britain (160), Italy (112), Germany (96), Belgium (48) and the Netherlands (48) (Frey 2010b:48).

In 1985 in the Soviet Union Mikhail Gorbachev came to power, replacing Konstantin Chernenko. Under Gorbachev's leadership the Soviet Union started to negotiate with the USA on the disarmament of the missiles. The negotiations led in 1987 to the INF (Intermediate-Range Nuclear Force)Treaty, which included the withdrawal and scrapping of SS-20, Pershing II and Cruise Missiles.

Two years later, in 1989, the East-West confrontation ended with the opening of the borders between East and West.

The Antiwar Movement: No New Nuclear Weapons

The beginnings of the peace movement can be dated to 1978/79 when it became known that the U.S. planned to deploy a neutron bomb in Europe (Carter 1992:112 f). This weapon -- of which it was said would largely spare inanimate matter but which would destroy all living things -- caused great indignation. The "Retrofit Decision" by NATO then worked as a catalyst (Risse-Kappen 1988:70). In Germany many new citizens' initiatives were founded -- in the cities often on a district basis. These initiatives joined forces with existing peace organizations and with organizations from the context of the churches and parties. The movement collected signatures against the missiles and from 1981 mobilized large demonstrations. In Germany the first large demonstration was in June at an event of the Protestant Church in Hamburg.

In the fall of 1981, 300,000 people demonstrated in the Bonn Hofgarten; 100,000 in Brussels; 250,000 in London.

In 1982, there were already 400,000 in Bonn (Risse-Kappen 1988:71). In the USA in 1982 more than a million people participated in a demonstration in New York's Central Park; 500,000 were in different cities in Italy (Cortright 2008:146 pp).

The climax of the protests was in October 1983 when NATO was preparing to deploy the new missiles. Overall, protest throughout Europe against the deployment involved around three million people, including nearly a million in The Hague (Cortright 2008:14). In Germany from the 15th October a week of action took place with the individual days dedicated to particular topics or social groups (eg., churches, women, businesses, educational institutions). The protests included a 108 km long human chain between Stuttgart and Ulm. Large-scale demonstrations in Berlin, Hamburg and Bonn on 22 October 1983 were attended by 1.3 million people. [35]

The protests reflected the mood of the population. Both in Germany and in the U.S. (probably also in other countries) an overwhelming majority of nearly three-quarters of the population (72%) spoke in the polls against the retrofitting of the nuclear weapons and in favour of a freeze on nuclear armament (Wittner 2007:8, Frey 2010a).

After the deployment of the missiles, the protests declined numerically. But until 1986 still many tens of thousands were further engaged against nuclear missiles. In Germany actions of civil disobedience, especially blockades of nuclear weapons' bases, played an important role. Blockades became for a few years "the" form of action of the peace movement. The campaign "Civil Disobedience Until Disarmament" mobilized several thousand people for sit-ins in Mutlangen, leading to 3,000 arrests (Schlupp-Hauck 2005).

35 Siehe www.friedenskooperative.de/netzwerk/histo000.htm .

A new large demonstration took place in 1986 in Hasselbach where Cruise Missiles were to be deployed and in which over 180,000 people took part.[36] In 1988 there was a demonstration at a planned NATO Headquarters in Linnich – Glimbach which saw at least a few tens of thousands.

The West German peace movement of the 1980s was varied -- spanning churches and church-related groups,trade unions, independent peace groups, student organizations, the independent Left (including the Kommunistischer Bund -- KB), parts of the Social Democratic Party SPD, the 1980 newly created Greens and left parties such as the Communists (DKP) and the DFU (German Peace Union, close to DKP) oriented towards the socialism of the Eastern Bloc (Frey 2010a and 2010b). Countless local initiatives emerged in cities, often at neighbourhood level. Leif (2001) estimates their number in 1983 at 4,000 to 6,000. In 1981 the peace movement created an umbrella, the Coordination Committee of the Peace Movement ("KA"). Representatives from 30 different groups sat in the Committee which was strictly adhering to an equilibrium of the different "spectra". These spectra, as they were defined at that time, were (Leif 2001): Social Democrats and groups close to the trade unions; churches and groups close to the churches; Communists; Green party; and "independent peace groups" that included among others the KB and the Federation of Nonviolent Action Group[37], a nonviolent-anarchist grouping. The KA was represented to the public by several spokespeople. In annual conferences of numerous activists of the peace movement, the respective next steps (e.g. new large-scale

36 Junker, Dietrich (o.D.) Frieden braucht Bewegung. http://www.fi-hunsrueck.de/FI/_contentdata/Gro%C3%9Fdemonstration%20Brosch%C3%BCre.pdf?PHPSESSID=67ee8e3e648ed832d8d634da4cf57bd9; Szech, Reiner (1986) Hasselbach: Über 180,000 Demonstranten vor Stationierungsort für Cruise Missiles, http://www.friedenskooperative.de/netzwerk/histo111.htm

37 For the latter the author attended some years the Coordination Committee.

demonstrations) were agreed under the direction of KA. Leif (2001) writes about the structures of that time:

„*At the beginning of the 1980s, there were multiple networks that organized themselves through regular meetings and conferences. These networks were based upon the [recently-established] regional or city-based peace initiatives as well as upon the [longer-standing] peace bureaus. On the level of districts, large cities and states, there were in addition further structures with identity particular to their own different states.*

With these structures the need of grassroots' groups for coordination and exchange was mostly met. The coordination at the national level (action conferences, the Coordinating Committee) was considered to be too aloof [for the grassroots] and was only of interest to the few activists who were familiar with the formation of organisational culture and mechanisms and could handle them.." (Leif 2001)

In the section on impact it will be made clear that the West German peace movement cannot be seen separately from what happened in other European countries and the United States. The effects it achieved were not accomplished as an isolated German peace movement but rather as an international effort. Organizations internationally established and influential were, for example, the International Physicians against Nuclear War (IPPNW) who were recognized for their commitment in 1985 with the Nobel Peace Prize. In the UK it was the Campaign for Nuclear Disarmament (CND) which was active in a broad coalition of peace groups against nuclear armament. In the U.S., there was since 1979 the "Freeze" movement, also supported by a number of organizations, including some which had been active in the 1960s (e.g, SANE) or even dated back earlier (Boulding 1990:19 pp). They quickly found much support. In surveys in 1983, 80 % of the population in the USA supported the freeze and also the oppositional Democrats made the claim their own (Pentz 1984).

Also in the GDR (East Germany) in the 1980s an independent peace movement was created although not numerically comparable to that in the FRG. It consisted mainly of church-related groups which, together with Western church groups in1980, created a "Decade of Peace". Ten days of November each year were devoted to the theme "swords into plowshares" (Oelerich 2013).

Bloc-crossing activities were operated also in the leftist environment. So-called Peace Councils from countries of the Eastern bloc met with peace groups from the West, exchanging experiences, proposals for detente and the prevention of further nuclear armament.

A highlight of such activities, organized together by the independent and quasi-governmental groups was the Olof Palme March from 1 to 18 September 1987. Initiated by the DFG-VK (a German section of War Resisters' International) together with the Peace Council of the German Democratic Republic and the Peace Committee of Czechoslovakia, the march led through the GDR. A report of the Gauck office (the office that deals with the Stasi files, the files of the East German secret service) says:: "*About 500 to 600 people, including many representatives of independent peace groups, participated. At the same time... they protested against nuclear power plants and the GDR environment and the demarcation policy. When the train carrying the pilgrims arrived in Oranienburg, the authorities ordered 5,000[government-directed] demonstrators to confront the train in order to break the dominance of the independent groups and their banners.* "[38]

The West German peace movement took very different positions with respect to many issues -- from attitudes to the ‚real existing socialism' in Eastern Europe and the Soviet Union and the issue of the SS-20, on through to the question of civilian

38 http://www.bstu.bund.de/DE/Wissen/Aktenfunde/Palme-Friedensmarsch/palme-marsch_node.html

usage of nuclear power and varying positions about whether civil disobedience actions were useful or counterproductive to different societal visions and utopian ideas about an ideal society. But the movement managed to bridge these differences through what was called a "minimum consensus". This minimum consensus was the rejection of the deployment of Pershing II and Cruise Missiles in Western Europe. It was written down in Germany in an appeal called the Krefeld Appeal.[39] By 1983 signatures to this appeal, partially collected by activists going door-to-door, numbered four million. (Frey 2010a).

Only after 1983 did the differences between the individual spectra became more apparent (Leif 2001). So-called independent groups and parts of the Christian groups increasingly focused on actions of civil disobedience. In 1984 in addition to the aforementioned campaign, Civil Disobedience Until Disarmament, a two-week camp in the so-called Fulda Gap took place. The activists aimed at disturbing manoeuvres of NATO forces at the border to the GDR. Their aim was to draw the attention of the public to the offensive elements of NATO's strategy.

The three main strategies and methods of the peace movement of the 1980s were the signature collection (Krefeld Appeal), annual mass demonstrations, and increasingly, as a third element, sit-ins in front of nuclear weapons bases. The latter began in 1982 with a first blockade in Großengstingen. After the deployment of the new nuclear weapons, the action "Civil Disobedience Until Disarmament" was launched. It focused on the Pershing II base Mutlangen and organized numerous nonviolent blockades, including the involvement of celebrities such as the writer Heinrich Böll and prominent members of parliament. Also at other bases, there have been sit-ins and other actions such as intrusions into military bases and against

39 Krefeld is a town in Western Gemrany where the meeting took place which created this appeal.

manoeuvres. Models for these actions were, firstly, the anti-nuclear movement, where there had been a first blockade in 1975 in Wyhl (see Stey 2004, Sternstein 2013); as well as the women-only camp in Greenham Common (England) lasting from 1981 to 2000; and at an RAF base where cruise missiles were to be deployed (see Hipperson n.d., Carter 1992:129); and also the blockades at the Italian base in Comiso, Sicily.

In addition to these three main forms of protest, there were other approaches and activities. The number of conscientious objectors increased significantly despite a temporary worsening of the recognition process and came to over 50,000 per year (in 1975 there had been around 30,000) [40]. Tax resistance, promotion of alternative forms of defence (defensive defence[41], civilian-based defence), and various imaginative forms of protest such as street theatre, open air concerts, etc., were also instruments of the movement.

Repression

Apart from the prosecution of civil disobedience actions, there was in Germany[42] little repression against the peace movement as a whole. This was different for members of the DKP (communist party) and its implementing organizations. Until the late 1980s the so-called Radicals' Decree was in force[43]. It decreed that all applicants for civil service (including teachers for

40 See: Kurze Chronik der Zentralstelle KDV, http://www.zentralstelle-kdv.de/z.php?ID=119

41 Military defence based on small and light weapons only that cannot be used for military aggression.

42 In Italy the police used violence against those who blocked the base in Comiso. 20 people were wounded seriously (see Carter 1992:129 pp)

43 The routine check with the internal intelligence service was stopped by the states between 1985 and 1991. See http://de.wikipedia.org/wiki/Radikalenerlass

example) had to be checked for their fealty to the constitution. The intelligence services zealously collected information on the peace movement. The demonstrations (and sometimes even the blockades) looked usually[44] more like large festivals. The police held back, and often it was plain to see that at least parts of the police officers stood on the side of the protesters.

Outcomes and Impact

After 1983, the overwhelming feeling in the peace movement was that they had failed because they had not prevented the deployment of Pershing II and Cruise Missiles. Although many activists continued to work for their withdrawal, many also stopped their activism or turned to other topics. Only looking back at this decade is there now a different picture. Had the peace movement really failed because the nuclear missiles were actually deployed in 1983? This question was asked at that time as well as today. Similar to the Vietnam antiwar movement, the effect of the peace movement of the 1980s is controversial, with scholars as alike with activists. For example, Andreas Buro, one of the leaders of the peace movement, wrote in 2005: "*The Bundestag has decided, contrary to the 'vote of the street,' [to proceed with] the deployment of medium-range missiles. It can be assumed, however, that the massive protest and the following nonviolent blockades in Mutlangen and elsewhere have made 'the entire political environment alert to the fears of the population.*" (Buro 2005)

But would there have been the negotiations between the super powers if the international peace movement in Europe and the United States had failed to condemn the madness of the nuclear arms race and demonstrated its dangers? It seems to be a common phenomenon in social movements that at the

44 One exception was the use of water canons in Bonn at the large demonstration 1983 when the demonstrators on purpose ignored the ‚banned mile' (a range around the parliament where demonstrations were forbidden).

moment they achieve their original goals (fully or partly) they do not recognize this as their success. That is because they have by then resigned since their claims have become "mainstream" and/or it is those in power who implement the change, not the activists themselves (see Moyer 1987). This was described above on the Vietnam antiwar movement and is again very clear in this case. The reference of critics that the movement did not succeeded in making Reagan directly change policy in the early 1980s seems unconvincing: „*For example, in his international history of the peace movement, Lawrence Wittner comprehensively examines the Nuclear Freeze Movement as transnational history, but in the process he gives the organization a degree of credit for ending the arms race that does not acknowledge the movement's failure to influence policy during Reagan's second term*" (Peterson 2011:3).

It can be assumed that the peace movement had influence on the start of negotiations on the withdrawal of medium-range missiles in 1986 and ultimately also to the end of the bloc confrontation in 1989. In addition, they certainly played a role in the decision of 1984 against the renewal of nuclear weapons of short range which were deployed in Germany and the approval of SALT II by Reagan. This is true even though this treaty on the limitation of strategic nuclear weapons, negotiated by Carter and Brezhnev in 1979, has never been ratified by the United States (Wittner 2007:10, Rohwedder 2010).

„*The peace movement played an important role in altering the terms of the debate about national security, as well as [altering] long-standing political alliances. Although the movement suffered an immediate defeat on policy, it won victories in rhetoric and political culture that conditions subsequent discourse and public policy. Within just a few years in the early 1980s, both major parties changed their positions on national security issues substantially*", writes Meyer (1999: 193). Similar are the arguments of Leif (1990:244), Carter (1992:149 pp) and Risse-Kappen (1988 and 1995). The latter called the eventual withdrawal of the missiles the „*late victory of the peace movement*" (Risse-Kappen 1988:168). Breymann (2001:257 pp) points out that members of the administration in the U.S. themselves admitted that it had been the international peace movement which forced the U.S. to the negotiation table.

Lofland and Marullo (1990) bring forward the thesis that the peace movement in the U.S. contributed to a number of changes:

- „*Changing public opinion of the Soviet Union from hostile – based on extreme fear – to neutral or even positive – based on a more cautious, live-and-let-live attitude;*
- *Increasing knowledge and awareness of the United States' important but limited role in an interdependent global order;*
- *Heightening public outrage over defense contracting fraud, abuse, and mismanagement, leading to more oversight and regulation;*
- *Creating scientific, cultural, and educational exchange programs with the Soviet Union;*
- *Slowing or reducing nuclear force modernization and defence spending increases that otherwise would have occurred;*
- *Preventing a new generation of weapons from proceeding through the research and development stage without careful scrutiny;*[45]
- *Forcing a reticent president to enter into arms control negotiations; and*
- *Influencing Congress to play a more active role in shaping foreign policy, hindering or blocking some of the administration's more aggressive initiatives.*" (Lofland and Marullo 1990:15-16)

The 1980s ended with the democracy movements in Eastern

45 Also the peace movement was quite successful, according to MacDougall (1990), to stop, through advocacy with members of Congress, the MX-missile which was meant to replace the Minuteman.

Europe and the collapse of the Eastern Bloc. For this, there are of course several explanations. An official reading, which is represented today by adherents of 'realism', is that the Soviet Union was exhausted in the arms race (see Zaborowski 2009 and Cortwright). Others explain the change alone by Gorbachev and his reform policy, and do not pay attention to what made the phenomenon of Gorbachev possible at all.

"*As with many other events in European history, including the outbreak and the end of the Second World War, interpretations of the end of communism in the East depend on which side of the Iron Curtain you sat. The West European version, which is also shared by the Russians, says that the wall collapsed as a result of Gorbachev's perestroika and the Soviet leader's attempts to overcome East-West divisions. A reading from Central and Eastern Europe is very different where it is believed that Gorbachev was forced to embark on perestroika because of the Soviet Union's dramatic economic situation and the rise of dissident movements in Poland, Hungary and Czechoslovakia, which rendered the costs of maintaining the Soviet empire unsustainable. There is also an American interpretation of the fall of the wall. According to this version, it was Reagan's uncompromising position vis-a-vis the Soviet Union and in particular the 'Star Wars' project that exposed Moscow's inability to compete in the arms race and thus forced political concessions from the Kremlin*" (Zaborowski 2009:1).

Zaborowski makes the point that the popular movements in Eastern Europe were a critical factor.

Probably all the factors played a certain role. But the shift in consciousness would hardly have been possible without the resistance in the West against the Cold War. Georgy Arbatov, adviser to Gorbachev, said -- and according to Bittorf (1990) was not alone in his opinion: "*The peace movement was an expression of the consciousness shift that has taken place in the West German population. That was a factor in our decision to choose Mikhail Gorbachev as new Secretary General who was an advocate of a dedicated course of détente.*" (Bittorf 1990)

Conclusion: The impact of the collapse of the Eastern Bloc in 1989 was not a goal that the vast majority of the peace movement pursued consciously, and parts of it would have been horrified that their activities had this outcome. Yet it is hardly conceivable to have happened without the change of consciousness of the 1980s (Breyman 2001 Cortwright 2008).

As did the antiwar movement on Vietnam, so also did the peace movement of the 1980s have far-reaching effects in terms of political culture. "Peace" became a topic with which large numbers of people identified, nuclear weapons have become increasingly problematized, civil disobedience (mostly in the form of nonviolent blockades) became a recognized movement instrument, the number of conscientious objectors rose sharply and political participation through citizen initiatives became a usual way of organizing (Breyman 2001, Leif 1990). And it was the structures of the movement created in the 1980s that were active in the subsequent peace movements (against the Iraq war and in Afghanistan).

The Women in White in Liberia

The antiwar movement of women in Liberia is documented by a few articles, a biography and a documentary film ("Pray the Devil Back to Hell"[46]).

Nonviolence Amidst a Civil War

Liberia was founded in 1822 as a project of former slaves returning from the United States. Of the country's 3.5 million inhabitants, dispersed among at least 16 different ethnicities, the descendants of those slaves had formed a numerically small upper class that had ruled the country since its formation. In

46 Reticker/Disney, New York 2008, www.praythedevilbacktohell.com.

1980, Samuel K. Doe came to power in a coup and ended the rule of that upper class of the descendants of former slaves. In 1989 with a force of 100 rebels of the National Patriotic Front of Liberia (NPFL), Charles Taylor marched from the Ivory Coast into Liberia with the goal of overthrowing President Doe. Doe was overthrown in 1989. A military intervention in 1990 by the community of western African States, ECOWAS, led by Nigeria, remained ineffective because ECOWAS quickly became embroiled as another party to the war (Schlichte 2002, Bekoe 2008). What followed was civil war between several parties and with shifting alliances. By the time of the Abuja II Accord in 1996 when the war came to an end it was apparent that the war that had been fought with great brutality and that sexual violence had been extremely common (Lindorfer 2009). In 1997 Taylor won the elections in 1997 with a huge majority. But in 2000 the civil war flared up again as new rebel groups -- Liberians United for Reconciliation and Democracy (LURD) and the Movement for Democracy in Liberia -- emerged. Only in 2003 was there a definitive truce[47] which was mediated by the Liberia Contact Group and ECOWAS mediators from Ghana, Nigeria and South Africa (Rosenbrock 2007, Gerdes 2011, International Crisis Group 2002). While the negotiations were conducted in Accra, Taylor was placed under indictment by the International Criminal Court after which he returned to Liberia. A delegation stayed behind to continue the talks, and though fighting broke out in the capital Monrovia the peace agreement was concluded. In 2005 elections were held from which Ellen Johnson-Sirleaf (Unity Party), who was close to the women's movement, emerged as the winner. in 2011 she was honoured along with the leader of the women's peace movement, Leymah Gbowee Leterin, with the Nobel Peace Prize. [48]

47 Consisting of the USA, Great Britain, France, Morocco, Nigeria, Ghana, the Economic Community of West African States (ECOWAS), the African Union and the United Nations.

48 Taylor was extradited in 2006 from Nigeria to Sierra Leone. At

The Antiwar Movement: Make Peace Now

As early as 1994 there were the first big protests against the war on the part of the Liberian population. Civic groups in 1994 organized a "stay home for disarmament" to demand the armed groups lay down their weapons (International Crisis Group 2002).

In 2002 the Women in Peacebuilding Network (WIPNET) that was part of the West African Network for Peace (WANEP) conducted a "peace outreach project". Pairs of women went into churches, mosques and markets with the slogan: "Liberian women, awake for peace!" (Gbowee 2011:126pp). They distributed leaflets and discussed peacebuilding with the women. These activities did not catch much public attention and they themselves did not approach the media. In December 2002 the Peace Outreach Project ended but a training for that project was the place where the Christian and Muslim women met who then became the "Women in White".[49] The two founders were the Christian Leterin Leymah Gbowee, who beginning in 2002 had mobilized an initiative for peace prayers with members of her Lutheran church under the name Christian Women's Peace and the Muslim Asatu Bah Kenneth, a police officer and member of a senior women's peace group (LWI) who had founded the "Muslim Women for Peace".

In Liberia there had also previously been a well-functioning network of women's groups who advocated for peace. [50] But

---

the end of April 2012 he was convicted by the ICC in Sierra Leone.

49 Sources for the following discussion are: Hansen 2009:152 ff, Gbowee 2011, "Pray the Devil Back to Hell" (film), Global Nonviolent Action Database.

50 The Mano River Union Women's Peace Network (MARWOPNET) that worked against violence in the border region between Liberia, Sierra Leone and Guinea, and the Liberian

the breakthrough was achieved only with the "Women of Liberia Mass Action for Peace" as the Women in White called it, comprising members of both main modern religions in Liberia. Gbowee's and Asatu's peace groups merged in March 2003 to become the Women in White and published an appeal directed both to the government and to the rebels to end the war. Their protests quickly turned into a mass action by women. In early April 2003 a permanent vigil began – five hundred to a thousand women, all dressed in white. They gathered each day in the city close to the fish market on a street that was used every day by President Taylor on this drive to the office. Their motto was: "*The women of Liberia want peace now*". On 11 April for the first time over 3,000 women gathered. Muslim and Christian women marched together, despite mutual reservations.

The women found support from the Inter-Religious Council of Liberia, to which both faiths -- the Liberian Council of Churches and the National Liberian Muslim Council – belong (Hansen 2009). The women stayed with their basic protest, careful not to engage in political debates about the government, but sticking with the demand to make peace (Gbowee 2011:138 pp).

On 24 April 2003 President Taylor invited them to a meeting with him at which they presented their demand for peace. They refused to directly address Taylor but rather directed their remarks toward the presiding chairman of the Senate, the only woman in the room (2011:141). [51]

On another occasion, the women also met with members of LURD, as these had a meeting with representatives of the

---

Women's Initiative (LWI) that organised strikes and protests against the war and for the inclusion of women in disarmament projects. See Gbowee 2011.

51 This event can be watched in the film „Pray the Devil Back to Hell".

Liberian Council of Churches (Gbowee 2011:143). And at yet another opportunity with representatives of the UN.

After meeting with Taylor, they continued their protests. Actions of the capital spread to camps of IDPs. In order to make their actions more varied, they also began picketing (Gbowee 2011:142). Much attention in the media was paid to an action invented by Asatu. According to Gbowee it was originally a joke and it is unfortunately not known if Asatu was familiar with the ancient story. In any case, the action showed itself to be extremely useful in giving the women media publicity. The women had threatened to enact the story first told of Lysistrata: A sex strike in order to force men to end the war. (Gbowee 2011:147).

When the contact group succeeded in initiating peace talks in Accra, a group of women went there to continue their demonstrations outside the conference building. Continuing into August 2003, they demonstrated daily outside the conference building and urged the delegates in numerous discussions to achieve a compromise to end the war. As the talks seemed to be bogging down -- the women were under the impression that the delegates had no real interest in progress, but on the contrary were enjoying the good life in Accra -- the women one day blocked the doors of the conference hall and thereby forced the delegates to stay inside to continue negotiating. At first the police threatened to forcibly remove the women. But the women's response was: Gbowee threatened to disrobe. Undressing in front of men would not only have been breaking a taboo but also would have meant a curse upon the policemen involved. Before the situation escalated, the women found understanding from the international mediator, the Nigerian President Abubakar. He prevented a delegate from clearing a way by force through the women and he also stopped the police from intervening. [52] This action was televised with much public

52 Gbowee 2011:161 pp.

effect.(Gbowee 2011:154). After this action, the climate of the negotiations changed. The negotiators became serious and two weeks later, after the international community increased the pressure of Gbowee's side by threatening to stop funding the negotiations, the deal was closed.

After return to their homes, the women were celebrated. In the following years they continued their work by involving themselves in the disarmament process. Initially, their support was rejected by the UN -- who considered themselves to be the experts. But after chaos broke out, the women were accepted as supporters of the disarmament of the various rebel groups.

Still later, the women participated in the elections by calling for women to register and to elect Johnson-Sirleaf. She would certainly not have become president if the women's peace movement had not existed. After two and a half years, the work of the movement formally ended.

The women involved were Christians and Muslim. The initiative was first assumed by women from the city, but soon many women from the refugee camps took part, thus including the rural population. They had recognition and support of the clergy of both religions. They kept a distance from the political parties at that time.

The women were unanimous in their central demand: the belligerents should finally make peace. Conflicts within the movement were, according to Gbowee, on the one hand between the older, more established women's organizations and their group. She regards it as a conflict between classes: „*They were the educated elite; we were the indigenous poor*" (Gbowee 2011: 144). On the other hand Gbowee writes of a large number of internal conflicts among the Women in White -- conflicts over leadership and also of personal relationships.

The central strategy of the women was to make their demand publicly visible to the warring parties. These should be influenced to end the civil war. The women took advantage of mediation of third parties, particularly the leadership of the faith communities. Part of their protests may be classified as civil disobedience actions -- their protests on the market were always in danger of being cleared by the police, and of course the blockade of the negotiating hall in Accra is an impressive example of a credible and effective direct action.

Repression

The women remained largely unmolested by the police. At least there is in the available reports no evidence of repression. On the contrary, it was reported that when there was a potential threat the women had a contact within the police who warned them if something was developing there. [53]

Outcomes and Impact

Through their protests in Liberia and their pressure before the negotiations -- and especially during the negotiations --the Women's Peace Movement of 2002-2003 has contributed to the fact that the negotiations came successfully to an agreement. Of course they were not the only ones to whom the peace agreement can be attributed. The international mediation and the pressure exerted by their influence have been unquestionably decisive factors. But the women made publicly clear to both sides that they were simply tired of the war, and they then forced the politicians to take the negotiations seriously. In the academic literature on the end of the civil war, the protests of women usually are not mentioned. But that is probably due more to the unfortunately common tendency to ignore civil society initiatives, not because they were ineffective.

53 The information however is too vague to build conclusions upon it.

The Iraq War 1990-1991

The movement against the Iraq war 1990/1991 (Persian Gulf war or Gulf War II[54]) has been documented in some academic articles (see the footnote below). In addition, the author has been using issues of the German magazine Peace Forum as an original source.

War for Oil or War for International Law?

On 2 August 1990, Iraq occupied Kuwait. After several months of sanctions and ultimatums, the United Nations legitimized action on 29 November 1990 with: … *authorizes Member States … to use all necessary means to uphold and implement resolution 660 (1990) and all subsequent resolutions and to restore international peace and security in the area* " -- which meant an attack to liberate Kuwait (UNSC 678)[55] A so-called "coalition of the willing" from 28 countries under U.S. leadership attacked two days after the deadline of an ultimatum set by the UN - with the aim to force Iraq's withdrawal from Kuwait -- expired on 17 January 1991. According to an opinion expressed in Wikipedia the operation "Desert Storm" was "*in terms of military equipment used and the level of mobilization of the warring parties... the most destructive war since the end of World War II, even including the Korean War in the comparison.*" [56] In addition, the war distinguished itself, as also noted by Wikipedia, by the unusual asymmetric distribution of the victims of war, by the unilateral decision of the war's end and by the high degree of indirect environmental damage (especially by depleted uranium). According to Wikipedia, on the Allied side 237 dead and 776 wounded, in contrast to between 3,000

54 The first Gulf War was the war Iraq-Iran in the 1980s.

55 http://daccess-dds-ny.un.org/doc/RESOLUTION/GEN/NR0/575/28/IMG/NR057528.pdf?OpenElement. Yemen and Cuba voted against the resolution; China abstained.

56 https://de.wikipedia.org/wiki/Zweiter_Golfkrieg

and 200,000 killed on the Iraqi side.[57] (The number of casualties on the Iraqi side is controversial. Most estimates range from 25,000 to 75,000 soldiers and just over 2,200 civilian casualties.) Iraq tried to escalate the war (probably to arouse sympathy among Arab countries) by attacking Israel with Scud missiles.

The Antiwar Movement: No Blood For Oil

The Iraq conflict flared up shortly after 1989 when most of the peace movement hoped for a "peace dividend" after the collapse of the Warsaw Pact and the end of the Cold War. In today's perspective, the Iraq War and the Kosovo war in Yugoslavia heralded a new era of Western military-based foreign policy, although in 1991 not yet recognized as such. The peace movement began to mobilize against the threat of war from the autumn of 1990.[58] Their common slogan: "*No blood for oil*". In several cities in the U.S. and in Europe the first major protests took place on 20th October 1990. On 1st December 1990, 10,000 protesters gathered in Boston. Also in Germany many activities and new initiatives developed during this period against the Gulf War.

The protests against the Iraq war were of short duration. There were hundreds of thousands of demonstrators in Europe and the U.S. in the fall of 1990 and in January 1991, with three "mobilization high points" against the war in the USA on the weekends 12-13, 16-18 and on 26 January 1991. Key events were the expiration on 15 January of the UN ultimatum and the beginning on 17 January of "Desert Storm". The protests were as large as at the time of the Vietnam War in the United States and of the peace movement of the 1980s in Europe, if not greater; although the war, perhaps because it was officially

57 https://de.wikipedia.org/wiki/Zweiter_Golfkrieg#Opfer_und_Verluste

58 For the following discussion, see Koopman 2009:59, Cortright 2008:170ff, Zunes 2011:358, Friedensforum Sonderausgabe 1/1991

sanctioned by the UN, was seen in some populations as legitimate (see also Zunes 2011). In Bonn on the 26th January 1991 200,000 people gathered, more than expected by the organizers. In the opinion polls however a great majority of at least two-thirds of the (West) Germans always expressed support for the war. [59] The main cause for the shift in opinion that apparently took place was the bombing of Israel by Iraq. The attack on Israel delegitimized the peace movement in the eyes of many people who before had been sceptical about the war (Koopman 2009:64).

In addition to the demonstrations of opposition to the war, particularly noteworthy was an action of interpositioning between the fronts by nonviolent activists, even if this action was eventually ineffective. The Gulf Peace Team (GPT), a British-American-Austrian initiative (see Burrowes 2000) organized from Christmas 1990 a camp in the desert between Iraq and Kuwait in the hope of being able to stop in this way the advance of American troops. They were welcomed by the Iraqi government, even though they tried to keep their distance from the regime of Saddam Hussein. But when the war began, the bombers flew over the heads of the 250 activists who then were evacuated after 10 days to Baghdad. The same thing happened to the German sister initiative "Peace in the Gulf " that first organized a presence in Baghdad, but then joined the camp of the GPT.[60] The evacuees began then to organize humanitarian aid (see Schweitzer et al. 2001, Appendix Chapter 2).

The peace movement ended with the end of the war, although some groups, especially from the United States, continued to monitor the situation and to protest against the continuing

59 Zwietracht im einig Vaterland. SPIEGEL-Umfrage im Januar (II): Die Einstellung zum Golfkrieg und zur Situation in der Bundesrepublik', http://www.spiegel.de/spiegel/print/d-13487434.html; see also Rohwedder 2010.

60 With the exception of few who stayed in Baghdad.

embargo, some breaking it by delivering aid to Iraq. These groups also played a role in the resistance against the second Iraq War in 2003 (see below).

The protests were primarily carried by previously existing peace initiatives, the majority of them founded in the 1980s (Koopman 2009:62) or even already active in the case of the U.S. from the time of the Vietnam War. In Germany there were also the Social Democrats (at that time in the opposition), Alliance 90/The Greens, the PDS (reformed former Communists from the GDR), trade unions and organizations such as Terre des Hommes and the environmental organisation BUND. Greenpeace backed the opposition to the war and took part in the protests (Koopmans 2009:63). Shortly after the war began, many students of school age organized spontaneous, decentralized protests (Koopmans 2009:64). Counter-protests of supporters of the war saw, at least in Germany, only a few thousand participants (ibid).

In the U.S., a coalition was created in which were included the many different groups from left to right (including anti-Semitic and fascist groups according to Zunes (2011:355 pp.)) In Germany altogether (according to Koopmans 2009:60 pp) 953,000 people took part in the protests; in France 494.000; in the Netherlands only 18,800.

The movement was in agreement to condemn the attack of the "coalition of the willing". The war was seen as a war for oil and doubts were expressed that without the massive economic interests (dependence of oil), the coalition would not have tried to restore Kuwait's independence (Koopmans 57 pp).

In the U.S., there was, according Zunes (2011:358 f), no sympathy for the regime of Saddam Hussein and therefore no ideological agenda in contrast to what parts of the movement pursued in the cases of the wars in Vietnam and Latin America. This is also true for Germany as can be shown for example when analyzing the speeches of the demonstration on 26 January '91 (Friedensforum 1/1991). In discussions it was, however, sporadically pointed out that Kuwait had previously belonged for a long time to Iraq and that Kuwait was ruled by a very repressive government.[61]

Two main strategies of the movement can be identified. The first was the public protest before the ultimatum ended against the actions of Western governments with the hope to move them to a waiver of an attack or, when "Desert Storm" had started, its cancellation. In France and the Netherlands, demonstrations were the main methods. Methods of protests in Germany were, besides demonstrations: vigils, protest postcards and nonviolent actions such as the blockade of U.S. military vehicles in Mannheim on 29 November 1990 (see ‚Aktionen gegen den Golf-Krieg', in: Friedensforum 6/90, p. 3). Koopmans (2009) has categorized more than a third of all protests as "confrontational actions", including strikes, blockades (including of the Frankfurt airport and various military bases) and occupations of military facilities (p. 62, 64).

The second strategy was the above-described intention of interpositioning by the Gulf Peace Team.

A third strategy was conscientious objection and support of those objectors. At the heart of this strategy was solidarity with those who refused participation. The author could not find indication that there was the distinct hope to increase the numbers of refusers so much that the war would have been impeded.

61 Memory of the author.

Repression

Soldiers who had in one way or the other escaped from the war effort were severely prosecuted and punished. In Germany alone, more than 100 soldiers went AWOL. Then there was the legal prosecution of people who had called for the soldiers to desert -- some of them were sentenced to fines or penalties. For others, the procedures have been finally dismissed. (Roggenbuck 1991, Gräbener 1991).

Outcomes and Impact

The antiwar movement had no discernible influence on the course of the war and its end. This applies both to the protests in Western countries as well as to the interpositioning of the Gulf Peace Team (see Burrowes 2000).

Zunes who analyzed the movement, names a number of factors that contributed to the weakness of the antiwar movement: effective propaganda by the participating governments, censorship of the press, falsification of reports from the battlefield, the small number of allied casualties, short duration, and the nature of the Iraqi regime (Zunes 2011:354). But he also identifies a number of errors of the movement. Namely: they had little knowledge of the region, there was a false comparison with the Vietnam War including a completely unrealistic prediction of the number of casualties on the Allied side, the preparation started too late, the concerns of Kuwaitis was ignored, and the movement was internally divided and split (see above). Once the war began and particularly in light of the attacks on Israel the vast majority of people supported it, regarding the war as largely being without an alternative. A survey at the end of the second week of the war in the U.S. says that 60 % expressed that they had lost respect for the antiwar movement.

The Iraq War 2003

(Gulf War III)

Though it is by now more than 10 years ago, the movement against this war is little documented other than by a chapter in the study of Cortright (2008). The description here has mostly been compiled using 'grey' literature and documents of the (German) peace movement.

Weapons of Mass Destruction: Not to Be Found

The second Iraq War[62] in 2003, two years after the start of the war in Afghanistan in 2001, stood on the one hand in the context of the "war on terror" proclaimed by the U.S. and NATO. But it was on the other hand justified by the alleged possession of weapons of mass destruction by the regime of Saddam Hussein. Since Iraq's invasion of Kuwait in 1990 the country had stood under heavy sanction by the U.S. and the UN. Those sanctions had cost, according to the UN's own figures, the lives of 500,000 Iraqi children (Sponeck 2002). Justification for the war was prepared by the claim that Iraq possessed weapons of mass destruction and that Iraq was obstructing the work of UN inspectors who were supposed to verify the possession.

The war took place without the approval of the United Nations, though the U.S. and the UK, who led a so-called "coalition of the willing", initially claimed that the war was covered by the UN resolutions on sanctions.

It began on 20 March 2003 as a combined air and ground war with the bombing of Baghdad and the invasion of ground

62 Or in Germany referred to as the Third Gulf war -- with the first Gulf war being the Iraq-Iran war in the 1980s.

troops crossing the border from Kuwait into Iraq. On 1 May 2003, the war came to an end with the conquest of Baghdad and the fall of Saddam Hussein. There were (and are today) continuing terrorist attacks and hostilities, including the illegal program of targeted killings by drones operated by the CIA. [63] The growth of ISIS in 2014 also is closely linked to this war. Only when former Iraqi officers joined this terrorist group, bringing many weapons with them that the U.S. had given to Iraq after their victory, did ISIS become powerful enough to control large parts of Northern Iraq and Syria. This second war on Iraq cost both sides a lot more victims than the war in 1991: 5,000 Allied soldiers and more than 10,000 Iraqi soldiers and policemen died. The number of civilian casualties is again controversial. Estimates range from 100,000 to one million, with the time after the official "end" of the war included. [64]

In the same year, 2003, a new Iraqi government was established by the allied forces. U.S. combat troops, however, remained in the country until 2010/2011.

Several European countries, including Germany, did not participate in the "coalition of the willing". They complained about the lack of legitimacy by the UN and the absence of clear evidence that Iraq possessed weapons of mass destruction. Other reasons were concern about the destabilization of the

---

63 In the UN-Resolution 1441 from the 8. 11. 2002, Iraq was asked to report on its weapons arsenals and give free access to UN inspectors. If Iraq disobeyed these demands „serious consequences" were threatened. On the 27 November 2002, for the first time since 1998 when they had left the country, UN inspectors started to work there. The Iraqi government submitted the requested report on its weapons programme but the U.S. called this report insufficient. Source: http://www.wissen.de/lexikon/irak-krieg?chunk=eskalation-des-konflikts

64 On the drone programme, see for example BICC et al (2013)

Middle East, the weakening of the efforts in Afghanistan and expected high follow-up costs by occupation and reconstruction.

The Antiwar Movement – Joined By Governments

The antiwar movement against the Iraq war in 2003 has remained until today the last great mass movement against war. It was carried in Europe and the United States by a broad coalition of peace groups, trade unions, churches and others, organizing themselves even before the war began in 2002. On 15 February 2003 there were simultaneous, coordinated protests in many cities, among others by the European Social Forum, including protests in London, Rome and Barcelona. In Germany a mass demonstration in Berlin of around 500,000 took place. Overall, it is estimated that about nine to ten million people took part in the protests. When the war began, they continued the protest, but they did not reach the same numbers.

Part of the movement in Germany staged actions of civil disobedience and organized the campaign "resist". This campaign started out with a pledge, in case of attack on Iraq, to launch actions of civil disobedience (Stay 2003). When the war started, blockades and other direct nonviolent actions took place. There also were calls on soldiers to refuse the orders. (see Friedensforum 1/2003).

As in 1991, the war came relatively quickly to an end. After the war, the movement fell apart, and the attempt on the part of peace organizations to transfer their momentum to the movement against the war in Afghanistan must be regarded largely as having failed.

The antiwar movement was supported by a broad coalition of different groups. In addition to the "classic" pre-existing peace organizations there were trade unions and many church groups

-- even the Vatican expressed criticism of the war. According to Wikipedia, a total of more than 70 European trade union organizations in 38 countries responded to the European Trade Union Confederation (ETUC) call to set a ”sign of peace” on the 14th of March 2003.

The resistance was, according to Cortright (2008:170 pp), particularly strong in countries where governments supported the war effort -- as in the UK, Spain and Italy. In Spain and Italy more than 80% rejected the war; in Turkey 86% rejected it. But even in Germany -- which did not join the “coalition of the willing” -- 80 % of the population did not support the war (2008:173 Cortright, Rohwedder 2010).

The protest also spilled over to soldiers of the countries that were involved in the war. As in the time of the Vietnam war, thousands of military personnel submitted an “appeal to redress“ to the U.S. Congress, demanding the withdrawal of troops (Cortright 2008:176).

Unlike during the Iraq war in 1991, there was little disagreement in the movement and,there were no attacks on Israel (which could have caused a change of opinion). There was agreement in the condemnation of war, which was seen, like the war in 1991, as a war for oil (and strategic interests). There was little sympathy with the system of Saddam Hussein, but clear references to the unlawful character of the sanctions which mainly hit the civilian population (see Friedensforum 1, 2, and 3/2003).

With regard to the methods of the antiwar movement there is little new that was not also practiced in the movement of 1991 and against the Afghanistan war. The strategy consisted of public protests expressing disagreement and appealing to the governments not to go to war, coupled with actions of civil disobedience and calls for refusal to soldiers.

Repression

The actions of civil disobedience in some cases met rather massive police response, and some of the participants in nonviolent blockades were prosecuted. In Germany, however, many court cases were dismissed (Singe 2003).

Outcomes and Impact

The antiwar movement failed to prevent or stop the invasion of Iraq. Nevertheless, it had political implications at different levels. The USA did not manage to anchor its official justification for the war in public opinion -- namely, the alleged existence of weapons of mass destruction. In February 2003, the U.S. withdrew a draft resolution in the UN Security Council and went along with their main ally, the United Kingdom, and a number of other countries (including some militarily completely insignificant, although they were promised war benefits for their participation). The U.S. and U.K. then proceeded without seeking a mandate by the UN. Cortright describes this as a "*major victory for the global antiwar movement*"(Cortright 2008: 174).

An equally great victory was undoubtedly the non-participation of a number of countries in the war: This includes in Europe: France, Austria, Germany and the Scandinavian countries. [65]

In Germany and Spain, the war had effect on the upcoming elections. Observers see a connection both with Schroeder's victory in Germany, as with Zapatero's in Spain (Cortright 2008:174).

65 https://de.wikipedia.org/wiki/Dritter_Golfkrieg#Verluste

Further Examples

In the literature, there are notes on other cases in which citizen action had an effect on war. They are named here briefly without their veracity able to be verified.

Other Cases Cited in the Literature

In an essay of 1934, the anti-militarist **Bart de Ligt** names several cases in which a war or participation in a war was prevented by "the people". Unfortunately, it has not been possible for the author to find independent data on the named examples. In "normal" historical works they are not mentioned. Researching original sources from the time would probably be the only way to check those presented by de Ligt's observations but that was not possible within the limited time frame of this study. De Ligt reported:

- 1909: Spanish troops were withdrawn from Morocco due to the resistance of the Spanish people against the war.
- 1914: the Spanish government wanted to join the war on the side of the Central Powers (Austria-Hungary and Germany). Anarchists and syndicalists formed a united front of a million people and succeeded in preventing the war from expanding into Spain. Spain is the only country in Europe, besides Albania and the Scandinavian countries, that remained neutral in the First World War.
- 1917: Argentina's entry into the first World War was prevented by protests of the workers. Argentina had remained neutral, as did some other South American countries. The Swedish Embassy in Buenos Aires served as a mediator for diplomatic dispatches for

Germany. The Entente Powers protested against what they saw as support of the German war efforts and put pressure on the Argentine government to stand on their side. In September 1917 Argentina decided to break off all relations with Germany. A British navy ship then went to Buenos Aires to increase the pressure on Argentina. And from the other side, the Argentine fleet was threatened by German submarines. In this situation, anarchist workers' syndicates in particular called for strikes. It also came to armed clashes between the army and workers; bridges were blown up. Finally it came to a general strike against the will of socialist trade unions. This caused a political crisis and the dissolution of parliament. Despite massive repression against the strikers, they reached their goal: Argentina did not enter the war.

- 1920: due to the refusal of British workers to transport war material, and due to the threat of a general strike by workers' councils (mines, transport and harbours), the British government was forced to abandon its plan to interfere on the side of Poland in the war against Russia.

A book by **Dülffer, Kroger and Wittich** (1997) deals with "avoided wars"' between major powers in the period from the Crimean War to the First World War. The authors examine primarily the state level, but mention the "*question of the conditions of war prevention and various pressures on governments... which can go through parliaments, public or any other pressure groups* "(18). According to their findings when crises arose in colonies, public opinions expressed in the mother [colonizer] country played a role in effecting the conflict.. However, the authors mention only examples where an escalation of conflict, not de-escalation, was created by public opinion. In their list of de-escalation methods in 33 cases investigated by them, they name only government measures and instruments.[66]

Another example of an action that may have influenced a government to decide against war comes again from the U.S. We quote here a report by the **U.S. Fellowship of Reconciliation** (FOR): "*In the fall of 1954 the Fellowship of Reconciliation launched the "Surplus-Food-for-China" Campaign, hoping to influence the United States government to send food relief to famine-stricken China. China had suffered a disastrous flood, leaving millions homeless and millions more facing death by starvation. At this same time, the United States had the largest surplus of food in its history, purchased by the government to support farm prices. … Through the "Surplus-Food-for-China" campaign, the* FOR *hoped to gain enough public interest to persuade the United States government to offer food to its enemy, rather than bombs. This was the Cold War period when there was great fear of Communism in the United States, heightened since the successful Communist revolution in China in 1949.*

The campaign focused primarily on sending tiny grain-bags to the president. Each bag had a label addressed to President Eisenhower, while on the white cloth of the bag was printed "If Thine Enemy Hunger, Feed Him — Send Surplus Food to China." The FOR *made these grain bags available to people across the country, who were urged to fill them with rice or other grain and mail them to the White House. The idea of the campaign caught the attention of groups all across the country. Women started a petition to collect a million signatures urging the President to send a "love gift" of food to hungry Chinese children. … The New York Times ran almost a full-column article about the campaign, with a photograph of the grain bag. The European press also carried the story. By October 1955 Fellowship magazine reported the Food-for-China campaign seemed to have run its course, while an offer by the US to send food to China was*

66 Germany however supported the war indirectly: by taking over tasks the allies fulfilled in other regions; by taking care of the security of U.S. barracks with 7,000 German soldiers; by continuing to staff the AWACS planes; and by allowing the allied forces to use German air space.

never made. The campaign initially appeared to be a failure even though it amassed enthusiastic participation from thousands of Americans. The FOR *national office sent out over 40,000 grain-bags with reports from Washington indicating that most of them appeared at the White House, together with numerous other letters and petitions. It is possible however, that the 'Food-for-China' campaign did have a political impact.*

Al Hassler, editor of Fellowship, would later write: 'Except for one of the accidents of history, the Food-for-China campaign would have appeared to be an imaginative, colorful failure, like many another. But the "accident" was in the information, provided confidentially years later by a former member of Eisenhower's press staff, that the campaign had been discussed in cabinet meetings simultaneously with proposals from the Joint Chiefs of Staff for the bombing of mainland China. The President, said our informant, asked how many of the grain bags had been received. When he heard that there had been over 45,000 plus thousands of additional letters, he ruled against bombing—on the grounds that if so many Americans wanted reconciliation with China, it was hardly the time to start bombing it!' (December 1975)".[67]

The Wars in the Former Yugoslavia

There have been several wars that are the subject of antiwar movements that were not examined here. For Germany of particular importance were in the 1990s, first the insidiously growing military intervention in the war in Bosnia-Herzegovina; a few years later the NATO attack on Yugoslavia in 1999; and since 2001 the war in Afghanistan.

67 These instruments are according to the authors: 1. Territorial, political and economic compensation, 2. Preventive or parallel direction of the crisis, 3. Cumulative weakening of the conflict, 4. Search for convergence (Alliance of opponents), 5, Politics of the strong arm (deterrence), 6. Military balance, 7. Trust building, 8. Continued weakening of the conflict through rules or institutions (21 pp).

Against the military intervention in Kosovo by NATO (and without a UN mandate, see Hänsel & Stobbe 2002) altogether hundreds of thousands protested in Western Europe, Eastern Europe and Russia. Especially rallies on the 1st of May, the international Workers' Day, were under the influence of the war. But those who condemned the NATO attacks were divided. The divisive issue regarded positions on the independence movement in Kosovo. One side criticized the NATO attacks but supported its result, the secession of Kosovo from Serbia. The well-known nonviolent activist and peace researcher Jean-Marie Muller wrote in 1999: "*For sure, the war declared on Serbia defends a just cause. But it does not suffice that a cause is just for a war to be just.*".

The other position, which was mostly to be found on the political left, shows little or no sympathy for the concerns of the Kosovo Albanians but focused on the criticism of NATO's action. Some went so far as to take the side of Serbia, calling the Kosovo Albanians "terrorists" and seeing the NATO attack as an imperialist coup against a socialist country. [68]

The War on Afghanistan

The NATO war on Afghanistan began on 7 October 2001, a few weeks after 11 September and was based on the alleged support of Al Qaeda by the Taliban regime. In Germany on the 13th of October 2001 there were demonstrations in Berlin and Stuttgart with altogether around 80,000 participants.[69] Subsequent protests in Germany, for example, were organized on the occasion of each term extension for the German army, but did not again reach these numbers.[70]

---

68 http://forusa.org/programs/riceforpeace/foodforchina.html
69 See for example the articles on the website of the Kasseler Friedensratschlags, http://www.ag-friedensforschung.de/themen/NATO-Krieg/Welcome.html
70 http://www.ag-friedensforschung.de/presse/2001-10-14.html

The peace organizations involved were the same that also participated in the protests over the Iraq war and the war in Kosovo. In Germany the war in Afghanistan was initially approved by a majority of the population under the influence of the attacks of 11 September and also out of a feeling of antipathy towards the Taliban regime (Wittlich 2002). However, in 2007 already 65% of the population rejected it and in 2010, according to a Forsa survey, 62% of Germans spoke for the withdrawal from Afghanistan. [71] The positions within the peace movement are not fully defined. Differences arose again and again, for example, in reference to the question of whether to request only unconditional withdrawal or to work for a peaceful solution including the Taliban in Afghanistan. What impact, if any, the protests had to do with the eventual withdrawal of international troops in the very last years is difficult to assess.

Military intervention in Syria

A very recent example of a prevented escalation happened in 2013. More than two years after the beginning of the civil war in Syria, the Western states, once more led by the U.S., Britain and France, seemed ready to intervene militarily in Syria when reports came out reporting the use of chemical weapons by the Assad regime. Though by now the situation has changed again, and while this manuscript was being drafted, several Western and Arab allies bombed positions of ISIS. At the same time, Russia, pretending to join their efforts, in fact seems to have started a bombing campaign in support of the regime. It is worth looking back at what happened in 2013:

President Obama at first (on 25 August 2013) spoke only of a 'thorough examination of the accusations and of all options'

---

71 To my knowledge, the movement against the Afghanistan war has not been researched and documented.

when the chemical attacks became known.72 One day later his foreign minister, in very strong words, announced a limited military strike.[73] France and Britain agreed and declared their readiness to join the U.S., if necessary without agreement by the UN Security Council. [74] Other countries (among them Germany) declared that they would under no circumstances take part.

But doubts quickly started to be expressed, not only by peace organisations in the U.S. and Europe. In the U.S. opinion polls showed that 59% of the population were against a military attack.[75] Even think tanks like International Crisis Group that are not known for promoting pacifist recommendations warned against a military strike as being dangerous and hardly in the interest of the Syrian people.[76]

The concerted action made an impact. First the British Prime Minister Cameron announced that he would only act if his parliament agreed. Then also Obama said that he would consult both chambers of his parliament. The vote in Britain ended

72 Umfrage: Immer mehr Deutsche gegen Afghanistan-Einsätze. http://www.spiegel.de/politik/deutschland/umfrage-immer-mehr-deutsche-gegen-afghanistan-einsaetze-a-497842.html, Freitag, 3.8. 2007; ‚Afghanistan-Politik: Deutschland kämpft mit dem Krieg.' Spiegel Online 15.4.2010. http://www.spiegel.de/politik/ausland/afghanistan-politik-deutschland-kaempft-mit-dem-krieg-a-689243.html

73 Tagesschau, 25.8.2013 [24.9.2014]

74 http://www.washingtonpost.com/world/national-security/kerry-obama-determined-to-hold-syria-accountable-for-using-chemical-weapons/2013/08/26/599450c2-0e70-11e3-8cdd-bcdc09410972_print.html [24.9.2014]

75 http://www.bbc.co.uk/news/world-middle-east-23795088?print=true [24.9.2014]

76 International Herald Tribune 5.9.2013, S. 5 (President says the world set a 'red line' [24.9.2014])

badly for Cameron: the majority voted on 29 August against a military strike.

The attack was originally assumed to be carried out in the first week of September -- before a meeting of the G20 Summit in Moscow. But the character of the impending attack became more and more unclear. At first the politicians had spoken of a short, perhaps 2-day, bombing of military installations of the Assad regime; but sparing the places which were assumed to store chemical weapons in order to avoid their release[77]. This would be a purely punitive expedition without real influence on the war. Later the U.S. Senate expressed its readiness to agree to a bombing campaign for up to 60 days with an option of extension for another 30 days. And foreign minister Kerry said also in a press conference on the 3rd of September that ground troops were not excluded if there was a risk that chemical weapons would 'fall in the hands of extremists', a statement he partly took back soon after. [78]

At the G20 summit in Moscow that ended on the 6th of September, the U.S. and Russia were not able to agree on a common position. It was an expression of the growing conflict between East and West (keep in mind that this was before the crisis in Ukraine) that all EU countries present signed a common statement in which they supported the plans of the U.S. to respond militarily to the use of poisonous gas in Syria. [79] Soon after, during its summit in Vilnius that directly followed, the EU announced that it appealed to President Obama to wait for the result of the investigations the UN had undertaken regarding the incidents.

---

77 INTERNATIONAL CRISIS GROUP -- Syria Statement. 2.9.13 [24.9.2014]

78 After Syria chemical allegations, Obama considering limited military strike. The Washington Post, 26.8.13 [24.9.2014]

79 International Herald Tribune a.a.O. [24.9.2014]

In the meantime, President Obama continued to find support in the two houses of his parliament for the military strike. The Foreign Committee had voted for it, but his hope also to win [a vote in] Congress seemed small. Not only was the majority of the population of the United States against an attack on Syria, but also the majority in Congress. According to media reports from the 9th of September Obama had the support of only 30 of the 425 representatives. [80]

In this situation President Putin announced an initiative to put Syria's chemical weapons under the control of the United Nations in order to destroy them.[81] The U.S. said that this was agreed between Obama and Putin during the G20 summit – though it cannot be ascertained if this was true. Assad gave his agreement to the proposal. [82] The same day, Obama announced in a very short speech to the nation [83] that he would not order an attack on Syria as long as Syria abided by the destruction

80 http://www.tagesschau.de/ausland/gzwanzig-russland112.html vom 7.9.13. The full text of the statement can be read here: http://www.whitehouse.gov/the-press-office/2013/09/06/joint-statement-syria [24.9.2014]

81 Ebner, Karoline (2013) Präsident in der Zwickmühle, tagesschau 9.9.2013, http://www.tagesschau.de/ausland/syrien3108.html [24.9.2014]

82 Rosenberg, Steven (2013) Russia's Nimble Footwork on Syria. BBC News 11.9.2013, http://www.bbc.co.uk/news/world-europe-24045650?print=true [24.9.2014]

83 Goldfarb, Zachary A. und Nakamura, David (2013) Obama Takes Syria Case to the Public in White House Address, Washington Post 11.9.2013, http://www.washingtonpost.com/politics/obama-takes-syria-case-to-the-public-in-white-house-address/2013/09/10/11b5356a-1a36-11e3-82ef-a059e54c49d0_story.html [24.9.2014]

of its chemical weapons. [84] The war was averted, and the UN started to take the chemical weapons out of the country.

This also is a case where the renunciation of military action cannot be attributed alone to the rejection by the population. But the refusal in both the French and British parliaments certainly played a role in the negative turn of American public opinion as well as in the Congress itself.

84 The speech is documented here: http://www.washingtonpost.com/politics/running-transcript-president-obamas-sept-10-speech-on-syria/2013/09/10/a8826aa6-1a2e-11e3-8685-5021e0c41964_story.html [24.9.2014]

Conclusions

What are the conclusions of these examples? We would like first to look again at the impact and then ask the question if there are clear factors to be identified which are necessary for movements to be successful.

On the Outcomes and the Impact

The seven examples described in more detail represent three types that tentatively can be identified:

a) Four movements directed against a war which the activists considered as unjust and that their government conducted abroad (Vietnam, Nicaragua, Iraq 1990/91 and Iraq 2003).

b) A movement directed against a civil war in its own country (Liberia)

c) Two movements directed against a war that was threatened but had not yet actually started: Sweden 1905 and the anti-nuclear peace movement of the 1980s.

In the introduction it was already stated that the authors had originally assumed that it would be possible to identify movements that were clear-cut cases of movements preventing or stopping wars, and others which as clearly had to be considered as having failed in the endeavour.

The result however is a different one: No movement can claim to have stopped or prevented a war by its own, perhaps with the exception of the early conflict between Sweden and Norway.

But some of the movements undoubtedly were necessary for a peaceful solution. In the case of Liberia the women had clear influence on the outcome of the negotiations. The peace movement of the 1980s was not able to stop the deployment of nuclear weapons but contributed to their eventual withdrawal a few years later. Also the antiwar culture that developed during that time certainly influenced the later decades.

On the other hand also the seeming "failures" -- meaning those movements that did not achieve, at least not at the short-term, their objective to prevent or stop the war they protested against -- influenced the conduct of the war (Vietnam, Nicaragua), perhaps preventing worse. And they had longer-term effects which among other things led to individual countries not participating in a later war (Germany in Iraq 2003). Especially obvious is this the case of Nicaragua where probably there would have been a direct military intervention by the U.S. if the movement had not been there. To what degree the two movements contributed to the end of the military involvement is controversial. At best it was one factor but not the only -- and probably not the decisive one.

Two of the movements were quite clearly without influence in regard of their immediate objective: the movements against the Iraq wars 1991 and 2003. There was however a difference between them. In 2003 public opinion in many countries was much clearer against the war, and this critical stance was also shared by some governments in Europe. Generally speaking, some of the movements had longer-term influence on later conflicts, Iraq 2003 being the most obvious example.

As shown in the individual case studies, these observations on impact are hypotheses that are not, by far, shared by all political scientists, politicians and activists of the cases in question. In some cases, such as the anti-Vietnam war movement, there are conflicting discourses about the role of the antiwar movements and its influence, both during the course of the war and in the war's ending.. The same is true for the peace movement of the 1980s. In some other cases (e.g. the Iraq Wars, the U.S. conflict in Nicaragua, the civil war in Liberia) we will not find in most of the mainstream literature about these conflicts the term "antiwar movement". In political science, particularly under the rubric of 'International Relations', the predominant focus on the actions of governments has made these scientists fail to look at the role that citizens may have played in influencing governmental action. Social movement studies exist mostly in a parallel world and are not heeded by these researchers.

Almost continuously, in terms of the effects to be observed, was the factor of delay. Hardly any of the movements studied (with the exception of the women's movement in Liberia) experienced immediately that their demands had been fulfilled. In almost all cases, it took several years. And sometimes by the time of the desired results, the movements were almost moribund or had shrunk to a few active nuclei. This applies equally to the anti-Vietnam movement, the movement against the Contra war, and the peace movement of the 1980s. This observation is indirectly strengthened by the fact that the movements that were dealing with only a short-lived war (the two Iraq wars) were initially ineffective and could only, at best, influence the participation of their own governments in decisions about their participation in [future] wars. In other words, they contributed to a shift in consciousness in the population . How this happened and how sustainable the effects on the officials who in future had to decide on war or peace, would be worth a study of its own.

Factors Contributing to Success or Failure

In the introduction, some assumptions and hypotheses were presented regarding the question of what factors contribute to a movement having success or failure. This study here is not a statistical study. For that the number of cases investigated would have to be much higher. What can be allowed in this section, therefore, is only to test the plausibility of the presumed assumptions and, if necessary, to formulate new assumptions where no confirmatory indicators could be found for what originally has been put forward.

On War

- Duration of the war / conflict: The assumption had been that movements need some time to develop momentum. This has proven itself on the basis of the present examples as plausible because the examples show that the movements needed several months, or even more than a year, until they were in full swing. The two cases where the time span between the alert and the start of the war was very short -- i.e. the two attacks on Iraq -- remained both eventually without any success regarding the prevention of the war.

- Number of victims on the anti-war movement's – i.e., one's 'own' -- side: The assumption was that the more casualties have occurred on one's own side, the greater would be the desire in the population to end the war. The minimization of casualties is what influenced government action, at least in Western countries, to a large degree. This observation is certainly true for the Vietnam War. Nevertheless, a comparison of the selected seven cases shows no clear relation. It may be that merely the fear of their own potential losses has an equally large influence on the strength of a movement than does the actual number of victims.
- Number of casualties on the opponent's side: The hypothesis that the more casualties on the opposing side, the more likely does a movement have the potential to create moral outrage. This could not be proven. What was observed, however, is that the warring states usually endeavour -- by minimal or false reporting

(that diminishes the actual numbers of victims) -- to embellish the picture which otherwise would lead to the emergence of outrage among the population.

- Geographical proximity to the war: Here the presupposition was: The closer [the war], the greater the concern. If it comes to geographical proximity, this assumption has proven to be barely plausible,: Vietnam and Iraq are many thousands of kilometres away from the countries where the main movements took place. It is probably not the geographical proximity that is decisive, but a perceived proximity – which is a feeling that can be aroused by many different things.

On the movement

- Duration of the movement: The investigated movements had varying durations, but they generally were closely related to the duration of the conflict against which they protested. Most but not all movements began with the escalation of the conflict – e.g., the growing secession movement in Norway, the announcement to deploy new nuclear weapons, the UN ultimatum on Iraq. The movement against the Vietnam War began only when larger numbers of troops were moved to Vietnam. And the Women in White in Liberia only became active many years after the civil war had started. There was no clear relationship between the duration of a movement and its successes. Impact was effected for both a very short movement (Liberia) as well as for two longer ones (Nicaragua and the anti-nuclear movement of the1980s).
- The movement of the women in Liberia was also where the number of active participants was relatively

small compared to the other movements which were considered influential. The reason for the special status of this movement is likely to be seen in the fact that they began at a crucial time – the 'window of opportunity', as is well-known in the field of conflict studies. The other movements contained large numbers but that fact was a criteria for choosing them as examples. So there cannot be a valid conclusion drawn. It would need a survey of all movements of a certain period to prove what instinctively seems plausible: That the size influences the outcome.

- Unity in goals: The assumption that unity increases the chances for impact, was put forward inter alia by Guigni (1999). This assumption plays a role in the analysis of successful nonviolent uprisings. On the other hand Jeffreys-Jones says in regard to the anti-Vietnam movement that it was the disunity of the movement that contributed cumulatively to the confusion of government. For two other cases, the role of "minimal consensus" was emphasized: Liberia and the anti-nuclear movement of the 1980s. So the picture seems unclear though it remains plausible that unity is important.

- Social diversity of members and supporters: This is one of the factors that has been worked out by the research on successful nonviolent resistance and nonviolent uprisings that have the goal of regime change. The importance of this factor was also reflected clearly in the investigated antiwar movements. The more successful among them managed to form broad alliances that reached far into what, in Germany, is known as the "conservative camp": i.e., moderate parties, churches, trade unions, professional associations. The Liberian

Women in White are a good example of that.

- Clear leadership in the movement: For the assumption that identifiable spokespeople or leaders are important for greater efficiency, there was in the case studies little indication that a central leadership is a condition of successful nonviolent resistance. One of the movements had very prominent leaders (Liberia), but in the others leadership was shared by a number of people and groups who acted as spokespersons but who did not play the same role as a Martin Luther King or a Gandhi in their movements.
- Tactical diversity, especially a modicum of civil disobedience or other direct nonviolent actions: The fact that a variety of forms of action -- including, in particular, direct nonviolent action movements -- lend weight, and thus increase the chance of impact, has not been substantiated. Using the example of women in Liberia one can see how a well-placed nonviolent action appropriate to the circumstances (the siege of the conference hall during the peace negotiations) did not fail to make a transformative impression. But in many other cases the nonviolent actions did not seem to be a decisive strategy leading to success. It would require more detailed studies of individual movements, in order to arrive at robust conclusions. The impression -- and it is nothing more than that – is, that from the descriptions of the present cases, nonviolent action was effective if the activists managed to connect to the overall movement and managed to awake understanding and support by wider social circles.
- Contact with government of the "hostile "or the attacked country: Here I wrote above, "both positive

and negative impact on the success of a movement can be expected". In the case studies, there were three (Vietnam, the peace movement of the 1980s, Nicaragua) in which at least a part of the movement sympathized with the "enemy" government. And at least in the last two there were direct contacts. And indeed there were both positive and negative impact factors. The two negatives were that, on the one hand, such contacts were controversial in the movements and contributed to their disagreement. And secondly, that in the wider population such contacts were considered to be aggressively critical, even as "treason", and helped those who sought to discredit the movement. On the other hand contacts under the umbrella of "citizens' diplomacy" also helped the movement, at least in the case of the peace movement of the 1980s. That was because it helped with mutual understanding and might have assured the government of the other side that there was a serious movement fighting for disarmament.

- Contact with people in the attacked country: Here the large and positive effects dominated, especially because such contacts allowed reporting of the suffering caused by the actions of one's own government, thereby arousing concern. This was particularly evident in the case of conflict between Sweden and Norway, where the international relations of the socialist workers' movement were an important factor. It was also an important facor in the case of Nicaragua where the many visitors, after visiting the country, organized information events back home in the U.S. and in Europe -- an important factor in the strategy of the antiwar movement. The same is true for those peace groups (often church-related) who had contacts to oppositional grassroots' groups in Eastern Europe. These contacts added to their credibility and allowed access to more conservative circles in the West.

- Constructive programs and humanitarian aid only played a role in a few of the movements. In those cases they seem to have increased the credibility of the movement (e.g., Nicaragua, Iraq).
- Level of violence: As explained earlier, there are different theories in movement research regarding the impact that violent actions have on the success of a movement. Those researching civil resistance emphasise the importance of nonviolence. In the investigated case studies the level of violence was low. Only in the case of Sweden-Norway was there quite a potential for violence among the anti-militarists. And also a rebellion in the military itself could not be excluded. The violence in the ranks of the U.S. military in Vietnam against superiors should not be considered as belonging to the antiwar movement though it was an expression of soldiers being tired of, and disillusioned by, the war.
- Support of the movement by other countries: This is another of the factors that have been derived from the study of nonviolent uprisings. However, in the movements studied it rarely occurred -- with the exception of the targeted support of the Western peace movements by Eastern Bloc countries (in the case of Germany, particularly through contacts by western communist factions to the GDR).
- From similar movements in other countries we have a different picture regarding the support of movements:

Several of the investigated peace movements acted in close coordination and solidarity. In the anti-Vietnam war movement this solidarity was only just in its infancy, but it played a major role in the peace movement of the 1980s, the movement against the Contra war and the two Iraq wars. In those cases there were not only parallel movements in several European countries and in North America, but these interacted also with each other and supported each other. However, the observation of Koopmans (2009:68) still holds true that, despite all the international networking, protest still primarily happens in a national frame of reference. The differences between the respective parallel peace movements in Europe makes this very clear. Especially strong was the coordination in the case of the Iraq war 2003. While no direct correlation to the success or failure of the movements could be observed, nevertheless such cooperation certainly strengthened at least the movements themselves.

- Level of sanctions (repression) and fatalities in the movement were aspects that did not have the same weight in the movements studied as in nonviolent uprisings that had the goal of regime change. This was true even if in some of the movements there were repression and casualties. Accordingly ambiguous is the effect of such pressure upon the success of the movement. There is although evidence in the case of the anti-Vietnam war movement and the legal persecution of nonviolent blockaders in the European movements that the disclosure of such repression brought sympathy to the movement. Brian Martin (2011) calls this the "backfire" effect of repression.
- The attitude towards the opponent in general --

and/or especially to the security forces -- is a point which was difficult to assess. In the case of Norway-Sweden it was obvious that there were many and close relations between the opponents of a war and the political powers in both countries. And that the socialists within the military threatened to revolt. A clear line of communication existed also between the women of Liberia and the political ranks. In the case of Vietnam, soldiers and reservists were an important part of the movement, and also in the Iraq wars there were appeals to soldiers to refuse to go the war and support for those who went AWOL. How much the movements tried to win over the police to their cause cannot be discerned from the secondary sources used for this study.

Context

- When elites are divided and groups who are close to the power centre of the country shift their loyalty, this increases the chances for success in the case of unarmed uprising (see Chenoweth and Stephen 2011). The same is clearly the case for the peace movements. Explicitly mentioned were those of Norway-Sweden, of Vietnam, of the peace movement of the 1980s and of the Iraq war of 2003. These were also not supported by part of some of the reigning European political parties. In that last case war was not prevented, but the decision by some governments not to participate in the war can certainly at least partially be attributed to the peace movements.
- Scandalous events and government wrongdoing (such as Watergate or the CIA deal with Iran during the

Contra war) have always given movements the tools to weaken the position of their government's move toward war. Such discrediting events strengthened the peace movements in the public debate.

Ultimately it seems that similar conditions apply for peace movements as for other movements and nonviolent uprisings. The available data base is, as said earlier, not sufficient to come to robust conclusions. But the individual case reports do indicate that movements rather have a chance of success if:

- they have time to unfold;
- there is an emotional shock and moral outrage among large sections of the population, no matter how this is triggered -- by a perceived threat, by the growth of the numbers of casualties on the population's side or by reports of atrocities committed by their own military;
- they include a wide range of social groupings;
- they manage to avoid -- through their own actions (whether violent or nonviolent) -- deterring potential supporters or the wider population;
- they find support among the (political) opposition in their own country;
- they appear credible in the eyes of large sections of the population as well as of the elites. This can be achieved through various measures and strategies. Their own diversity plays just as important a role as constructive or humanitarian programs. The means used make people understand their actions (usually more effective with nonviolent actions than with violent ones), as does the long-term commitment of the engagement.

Conclusion

In comparison to other social movements peace or antiwar movements seem to be those for whom success seems the hardest. Numerous social movements in other areas, from the women's movement to the environmental movement, from movements that take care of specific local concerns to nonviolent uprisings … these all have had many successes in the last hundred years. In peace movements however -- and despite the author's attempt to specifically select some "successful" movements -- an undeniable contribution to the desired result was achieved only in the historically very early example of Norway-Sweden. For the others, there was only (but also at least) an incontestable indication that they did contribute to the result that they aimed at. So what is special about peace movements, in contrast to other movements?

We would hypothesize that the comparatively small chance of success for movements seeking to prevent or end a war is due to two reasons. Firstly, issues of war and peace are issues that affect the core identity of states (see Krippendorff 1985). Because yielding would probably be seen as a direct threat to national security, they are therefore subjects where compromise or the yielding of a government is the hardest to reach. Secondly, wars tend to throw many people into a maelstrom of emotions – sentiments of threat and of patriotism oscillating wildly on all sides. To oppose one's soldiers and one's own government in the event of war is -- not only in the western cultural area – widely seen as treason and considered with contempt. "Right or wrong, my country" is a mindset which, in the last twenty or thirty years, the Western peace movements have partly succeeded to question. This already constitutes of itself a remarkable achievement though it was not sufficient to prevent those wars discussed here. To ask citizens to form their own opinion on issues of foreign policy and to the use of military action is something that has become more acceptable in the last three decades. A number of international and national organisations have achieved -- through public declarations of commitment, signature collections, media campaigns and information events -- that a larger number of people has started to feel responsibility regarding these questions. It would be interesting to research further into the influences that have contributed to such changes in behaviour and attitude. For example: To what degree can such a change in society be proven? How much is influenced by economic developments? To what degree are historical memories (like the Holocaust and colonialism) experienced as transgenerational trauma? [85]

As with conflict transformation in general, the problem with research on impact is to demonstrate effects of actions that will prevent an event from occurring. Jørgen Johansen commented on the value of counterfactual history in his chapter on Norway-Sweden. It is necessary to remember: The Cold War did not lead to a third world war, although such a war was, without any doubt, possible. How many more wars might there have been if it had not been for the antiwar movements as they have been formed since the 1960s in North America and Western Europe? Maybe when one day the government archives of the last decades are opened, researchers will find that there were some situations where governments were toying with the idea of war but, given the fear that their actions would encounter much opposition in the population, decided not to pursue that option.

In this paper we studied and compared quite different movements. As part of a larger scientific study it would make sense to form several categories and consider each category of conflict separately. But given the limited scope of this study it seemed very inviting to consider peace movements in different contexts to see whether there were clear contextual commonalities in terms of the effects of the movements.

85 ibid

With the exception of the early Scandinavian case which was a case of successful war prevention, some of the movements against wars impacted both the conduct of the conflict and its eventual end. But none of them could be attributed with stopping it alone. Besides this result, evidence was found that the respective movements had a long-term influence on public opinion and helped to raise public awareness on issues of wars and so-called "humanitarian interventions". This had an influence on later crises and how governments dealt with them in regard to engaging or not engaging in war.

The bottom line: Despite all the ambiguities of the attribution of effects and despite the special difficulties faced by peace movements: It is not true that peace movements have never prevented or stopped a war; or that they did not at least contribute to the prevention, deescalation or ending of them.

Literature

Aboagye & Bah (2005) 'Introduction'. In: Aboagye, Festus and Bah, Alhaji M. S. (Hrsg.) (2005) *A Tortuous Road to Peace. The Dynamics of Regional, UN and International Humanitarian Interventions in Liberia.* Pretoria: Institute for Security Studies, S. 1-10

Ackerman, Peter & Duvall, Jack (2000) *A Force More Powerful: A century of nonviolent conflict.* New York: St. Martin's Press

Ackerman, Peter & Kruegler, Christopher (1994) *Strategic Nonviolent Conflict: The Dynamics of People Power in the Twentieth Century.* Westport / London: Praeger

Adams, Nina S. (1992) 'The Women Who Left Them Behind'. In: Small and Hoover (Hrsg.) 1992:182-195

Anderson, Terry H. (1992) ‚The GI Movement and the Response from the Brass'. In: Small and Hoover (Hrsg.) 1992, S. 93-115

Arnoldson, Klas Pontus. P. (1892) *Pax mundi : a concise account of the progress of the movement for peace by means of arbitration, neutralization, international law and disarmament : authorized English edition,* London

Åselius, Gunnar (2005) 'Stormakterna och unionsupplösningen 1905'. In: Nilsson & Sørensen (Hrsg.) 2005: p 59-80

Balkan Peace Team (1996/1997) *Protests in Belgrade and throughout Yugoslavia—1996/1997.* From the Balkan Peace Team, Belgrade, 10 December 1996 and, part II, 23 January 1997. Online: www.hartford-hwp.com/archives/62/063.html [16.7.2008]

Barnes, Catherine (2007) ‚CSOs, Peacebulding and the Power of Partnerships'. In: van Tongeren, Paul und van Empel, Christine (Hrsg.) (2007) *Joint Action for Prevention. Civil Society and Government Cooperation on Conflict Prevention and Peacebuilding.* European Centre for Conflict Prevention. [Online] bei http://conflict-prevention.net [9.9.2008], S. 11-15

Bekoe, Dorina A. (2008) *Implementing Peace Agreements. Lessons from Mozambique, Angola and Liberia.* New York: Palgrave

Benedict, Hans-Jürgen (1977) 'Vom Protest zum Widerstand. Die Vietnamkriegs-Opposition in den USA und in der BRDÄ'. In: Steinweg, Reiner (Hrsg.) *Die Friedensbewegung.* Friedensanalysen für Theorie und Praxis Bd. 4, Frankfurt/Main: Suhrkamp Verlag, S. 79-106

Benner, Thorsten und Blume, Till (2009) ‚'Ma Ellen': Afrikas erste Präsidentin kämpft für den Wiederaufbau des kriegsverwüsteten Landes Liberia'. In: Evangelisches Missionswerk in Deutschland (Hrsg.) 2009, S. 13-23

Berg, Roald (2005) ‚Krigsplaner och yrkesmilitärens hållning 1890-1905', in: Nilsson & Sørensen (Hrsg.) 2005: 225-244

Beyna, Larry S.; Lund, Michael; Stacks, Stacy S.; Tuthill, Janet und Vondal, Patricia (2001) *The Effectiveness of Civil Society Initiatives in Controlling Violent Conflicts and Building Peace: A Study of Three Approaches in the Greater Horn of Africa. Synthesis Report on Key Findings and Lessons for Improving Practice.* Hrsg.: Management Systems International. [Online] bei < www.usaid.gov/regions/afr/conflictweb/pbp_report.pdf> [9.9.2008]

BICC, FEST, IFSH, HSFK (2013) *Friedensgutachten 2013.* Hrsg. Marc von Boemcken, Ines-Jacqueline Werkner, Margret Johannsen und Bruno Schoch. Berlin: Lit Verlag

Bittorf, Wilhelm (1990) ‚Giftgas ging, Unrecht bleibt.' DER SPIEGEL 44/1990, S. 72-77

Blom, Ida (2005) ‚1905 -- ett glädjens år'. In: Nilsson & Sørensen (Hrsg.) 2005, S. 109-126

Børresen, J. & Kristiansen, Tom (2005) *Levende breve fra de dødes rige. Admiral U. J. R. Børresens dagboksopptegnelser 1896–1910,* Bergen, Eide Forlag.

Børresen, Jacob (2004) 'Sjømilitære krigsforberedelser i ytre Oslofjord sommeren 1905'. *Borreminne*, S. 108-131.

Børresen, Jacob (2005) Admiralstriden 1905-1909. *Borreminne*, p. 94-121.

Boulding, Elise (1990) 'The Early Eighties Peak of the Peace Movement'. In: Marullo & Lofland 1990, S. 19-36

Boutros-Ghali, Boutros (1992) *An Agenda For Peace. Preventive Dipomacy, Peacemaking and Peacekeeping. Report of the Secretary-General pursuant to the statement adopted by the Summit Meeting of the Security Council on 31 January 1992.* New York: United Nations

Brock, Peter und Young, Nigel (1999) *Pacifism in the Twentieth Century.* Syracuse: Syracuse University Press

Burch, Stuart (2005) 'Norway and 1905'. *History Today,* 55, 2-3

Buro, Andreas (2005) *Die Friedensbewegung in der Bundesrepublik in ihren historischen Etappen.* www.friedenskooperative.de/netzwerk/histo114.htm [2.8.2013]

Burrowes, Robert J., 'The Persian Gulf War and the Gulf Peace Team'. In: Moser-Puangsuwan & Weber 2000, S. 305-316

Burstein, Paul (1999) 'Social Movements and Public Policy.' In: Giugni, Marco; McAdam, Doug and Tilly, Charles (Hrsg.) *How Social Movements Matter.* Minneapolis/London: University of Minnesota Press, S. 3-21

Burstein, Paul und Freudenburg, William (1982) 'Ending the Vietnam War: Components of Change in Senate Voting on Vietnam War Bills'. In: American Journal of Sociology Vol 82, No 5, S. 991-1006

Carter, Jimmy, April (1992) *Peace Movements. International Protest and World Politics Since 1945*. London & New York: Longman

Carter, Jimmy, April (2011) ‚People Power and Protest: The Literature on Civil Resistance in Historical Context'. In: Roberts & Ash, Timothy Garton (eds.) (2011^2), S. 25-42

Carter, Jimmy April (2012) *People Power and Political Change. Key Issues and Concepts.* London / New York: Routledge

Centre for Applied NonViolent Action & Strategies (2008) *10 Years of Nonviolent Conflict in Serbia.* Online: www.canvasopedia.org/content/serbian_case/nvc-serbia.htm [16.7.2008]

Chatfield, Charles (1990) 'The Antiwar Movement and America.' In: DeBenedetti 1990, S. 387-408

Chenoweth, Erica und Stephan, Maria J. (2011): *Why Civil Resistance Works. The Strategic Logic of Nonviolent Conflict.* New York: Colombia University Press

Chossudovsky, Michel (2006) 'NATO's War of Aggression in Yugoslavia: Who are the War Criminals?' In: Global Research, March. [Online] available from www.globalresearch.ca/index.php?context=va&aid=2144 [7.6.2008]

Chrisholm, Hugh (1911) *Encyclopædia Britannica* (11 ed.). Cambridge: Cambridge University Press

Cortright, David (1992) 'GI Resistance During the Vietnam War'. In: Small and Hoover (Hrsg.) 1992, S. 116-128

Cortright, David (2008) *Peace. A History of Movements and Ideas.* Cambridge: Cambridge University Press

Danielsen, Rolf (2005) ‚På moderationens grund. Några rättsliga och konstitutionella betraktelser över unionsupplösningen'. In: Nilsson & Sørensen (Hrsg.) 2005, S. 247-266

Davies, Philip (1989) 'U.S. Presidential Election Campaigns in the Vietnam Era'. In: Dumbrell 1989, S. 124-136

De Ligt, Bart (1934) 'Efficacité de l'action directe. Des exemples probants'. In: La Patrie Humaine 12. Januar 1934, S. 2-3

DeBenedetti, Charles, with Charles Chatfield (1990) *An American Ordeal. The Antiwar Movement of the Vietnam Era.* New York: Syracuse University Press

Della Porta, Donatella; Kriesi, Hanspeter and Rucht, Dieter (Hrsg.) (2009[2]) *Social Movements in a Globalizing World.* Basingstroke: Palgrave Macmillan

Dieterich, Johannes (2012) ‚Das Ende des Kriegsfürsten'. In: Frankfurter Rudnschaun, 26.4.2012, www.fr-online.de/politik/charles-taylor-vor-gericht-das-ende-des-kriegsfuersten,1472596,14993274.html [16.8.2013]

Due-Nielsen, Carsten (2005) ‚Danmark levererade kungen'. In: Nilsson & Sørensen (Hrsg.) 2005: 91-106

Due-Nielsen, Carsten (2005) ‚Danmark levererade kungen'. In: Nilsson & Sørensen (Hrsg.) 2005, S. 91-106

Dülffer, Jost ; Kröger, Martin und Wippich, Rolf-Harald (1997) *Vermiedene Kriege : Deeskalation von Konflikten der Großmächte zwischen Krimkrieg und Erstem Weltkrieg, 1865–1914.* Hrsg. Militärgeschichtliches Forschungsamt. München : R. Oldenbourg Verlag

Dumbrell, John (1989a) 'Introduction'. In: Dumbrell 1989, S. 1-6

Dumbrell, John (1989b) 'Congress and the Antiwar Movement'. In: Dumbrell 1989, S. 101-112

Dumbrell, John (Hrsg.) (1989) *Vietnam and the Antiwar Movement. An International Perspective.* Aldershot u. a.: Avebury

Echols, Alice (1992) 'Women Power and Women's Liberation. Exploring the Relationship Between the Antiwar Movement and the Women's Liberation Movement'. In: Small and Hoover (Hrsg.) 1992, S. 171-182

Evangelisches Missionswerk in Deutschland (Hrsg.) (2009) *Liberia. Land der Freien – Last der Freiheit.* Hamburg:EMW

Farber, David (1992) ‚'The Counterculture and the Antiwar Movement'. In: Small and Hoover (Hrsg.) 1992, S. 7-21

Fernström, Karl (1950) *Ungsocialismen : en krönika,* Stockholm, Federativs förl.

Fogelström, Per Anders (1971) *Kampen för fred. Berättelsen om en okänd folkrörelse,* Stockholm, Bonnier.

Försvarsstaben, Krigshistoriska Avdelningen (1958) *Militärt kring 1905 : en skildring av militära förberedelser och åtgärder i samband med unionskrisen,* Stockholm

Frey, Ulrich (2010a) ‚Die Friedensbewegung der 1980er Jahre'. In: Friedensforum 13F/2010, S. 28 -30

Frey, Ulrich (2010b) *Welche Rolle spielte die Friedensbewegung für den Fall der Mauer 1989 und das Ende der Blockkonfrontation?* www.frieden-schaffen.de/fix/dokumente/Welche%20Rolle%20spielte%20die%20%20Friedensbewegung%20f%FCr%201989%20und%20Ende%20der%20Blockkonforntation.pdf [21.3.2013]

FriedensForum 5-6/2001 bis 2/2013

Friedrich, Rudi (1995) 'Internationales Deserteursnetzwerk'. In: Wette, Wolfram (Hrsg.) (1995) *Deserteure der Wehrmacht.* Hrsg. Wette, Wolfram. Essen:Klartext Verlag, S: 333-355

Friedrich, Rudi. (1996) 'Arbeit mit Deserteuren und Kriegsdienstverweigerern'. In: *Jenseits der Gewalt. Arbeit für den Frieden in Ex-Jugoslawien.* Hrsg. Pax Christi. Idstein:Komzi-Verlag, S. 187-192

Gäfvert, B. (2005) ,Unionskrisen -- det svenska spioneriets pionjärtid'. In: Nilsson & Sørensen (Hrsg.) 2005: p. 207-224

Gäfvert, Björn. (2005) ,Unionskrisen -- det svenska spioneriets pionjärtid'. In: Nilsson & Sørensen (Hrsg.) 2005, S. 207-224

Gamson, William (1990) *Strategy of Social Protest.* Belmont: Wadsworth

Gamson, William A. (2003) ,Defining Movement „Success"'. In: Goodwin, Jeff & Jasper, James M. (Hrsg.) (2003) *The Social Movements Reader. Cases and Concepts.* Malden et al: Blackwell Publishers

Garfinkle, Adam (1997) *Telltale Hearts. The Origins and Impact of the Vietnam Antiwar Movement.* New York: St. Martin's Griffin

Gbowee, Leymah, with Carol Mithers (2011) *Mighty Be Our Powers. How Sisterhood, Prayer, and Sex Changed a Nation at War.* New York: Beast Books

Gerdes, Felix (2011) *Liberia's Post-War Elite. A New Era of Inclusive Ownership or Old Wine in New Bottles?* Arbeitspapier 1/2011 des Instituts für Politikwissenschaft an der Universität Hamburg. www.sozialwiss.uni-hamburg.de/publish/Ipw/Akuf/publ/AP2011-1.pdf [24.4.2012]

Giugni, Marco (1999) 'Introduction. How Social Movements Matter: Past Research, Present Problems, Future Developments.' In: Giugni, Marco, McAdam, Doug and Tilly, Charles (Hrsg.) *How Social Movements Matter.* Minneapolis/London: University of Minnesota Press: xiii-xxxiii

Gjelsvik, Nikolaus (1905) 'Rigsakten som traktat.' In: Samtiden, 69-81

Global Nonviolent Action Database http://nvdatabase.swarthmore.edu/content/liberian-women-act-end-civil-war-2003

Goers, Oliver (o.D.) *Geschichte der bundesdeutschen Friedensbewegung.* Berlin: Arbeitskreis für Friedenspolitik – Atomwaffenfreies Europa

Gräbener, Martin (1991) ,Der juristische Wüstensturm', Friedensforum 5/1991, S. 4-5.

Graf Sponeck, Hans C. (2002) ‚Die Sanktionen gegen den Irak sind ein Verstoß gegen die Genozid-Konvention. Die Lebensumstände der irakischen Bevölkerung sind erbärmlich.‘ Frankfurter Rundschau 7.2.2002, www.ag-friedensforschung.de/regionen/Irak/sponeck3.html [16.8.2012]

Griffin-Nolan, Ed (1991) *Witness for Peace. A Story of Resistance.* Louisville: Westminster / John Knox Press

Griffin-Nolan, Ed (2000) 'Witness for Peace'. In: Moser-Puangsuwan, Yeshua und Weber, Thomas (Hrsg.) *Nonviolent Intervention Across Borders, A Recurrent Vision.* Honolulu: Spark M. Matsunaga Institute for Peace, S. 279-304

Hagen, Nils Ole (2002) *„Misforståelsene i 1905. Norsk og svensk arbeiderbevegelses samarbeid i unionskonflikten i 1905.* Hovedfag, University of Oslo

Hall, Mitchell K. (1992) ‚CALCAV and Religious Opposition to the Vietnam War‘. In: Small and Hoover (Hrsg.) 1992, S. 35-52

Hammar, Inger (2004) *För freden och rösträtten : kvinnorna och den svensk-norska unionens sista dagar,* Lund, Nordic Academic Press.

Hammar, Inger 2005. ‚Krig eller fred år 1905? Den svensk-norska unionsupplösningen ur ett kvinnoperspektiv.‘ *RIG -- Kulturhistorisk tidskrift,* S. 88, 80-99

Hänsel, Heiko und Stobbe, Heinz-Günter (2002) *Die deutsche Debatte um den Kosovo-Krieg: Schwerpunkte und Ergebnisse. Versuch einer Bilanz nach drei Jahren.* Berlin: Heinrich-Böll-Stiftung, S. 86 ff

Hansen, Reinhard (2009) ‚Die Rolle der Kirchen in den Kriegen Liberias‘. In: Evangelisches Missionswerk in Deutschland (Hrsg.) 2009, S. 149-158

Heinemann-Grüder, Andreas und Bauer, Isabella (Hrsg.) (2013) *Zivile Konfliktbearbeitung. Vom Anspruch zur Wirklichkeit.* Opladen / Berlin / Toronto: Barbara Budrich

Hipperson, Sarah (n.d.) *Greenham Common Women's Peace Camp. 1981–2000.* www.greenhamwpc.org.uk/[3.7.2012]

Holl, Karl (1988) *Pazifismus in Deutschland.* Edition Suhrkamp

Horkildsen, D. (2005) Kyrkan och 1905. In: Nilsson & Sørensen (Hrsg.) 2005: p. 181-204

Howard, Donna (2001)'2.2.1 Peace Teams', .In: Schweitzer, Christine, Howard, Donna, Junge, Mareike, Levine, Corey, Stieren, Carl and Wallis, Tim (2001) *Nonviolent Peaceforce Feasibility Study.* < www.nonviolentpeaceforce.org/nonviolent-peaceforce-feasibility-study > [3.7.2012]

International Crisis Group (2002) *Liberia: The Key to Ending Regional Stability.* Africa Report N° 43, Freetown/Brussels

Isserman, Maurice (1992),You Don't Need a Weatherman but a Postman Can be Helpful'. In: Small and Hoover (Hrsg.) 1992, S. 22-34

Jeffreys-Jones, Rhodri (1999) *Peace Now! American Society and the Ending of the Vietnam War.* New Haven / London: Yale University Press

Jungar, Sune (2005) 'Finländska opinioner kring en union i upplösning.'. In: Nilsson & Sørensen (Hrsg.) 2005, S. 81-90

Jürgs, Michael (2005) *Merry Christmas. Der kleine Frieden im Großen Krieg.* München: Goldmann

Kolb, Felix (2005) *Protest, Opportunities, and Mechanisms. A Theory of Social Movements and Political Change.* Inaugural-Dissertation zur Erlangung des Doktorgrades am Fachbereich Politik-und Sozialwissenschaften der Freien Universität Berlin. Unpublished Ph. D thesis, Berlin

Koopman, Ruud (2009) 'Globalization or Still National Politics? A Comparison of Protests against the Gulf War in Germany, France, and the Netherlands'. In: Della Porta, Donatella; Kriesi, Hanspeter and Rucht, Dieter (Hrsg.) (2009[2]) *Social Movements in a Globalizing World.* Basingstroke:Palgrave Macmillan, S. 57-70

Krippendorff, Ekkehart (1985) *Staat und Krieg. Die historische Logik politischer Unvernunft*, Frankfurt a.Main:edition suhrkamp

Küchenmeister, Thomas (2010) ‚Die Konventionen zum Verbot von Landminen und Streumunition. Ein Erfolg der Zivilgesellschaft?!'. In: Friedensforum 1/2010, S. 39–41

Kvinneaksjon for unionsoppløsning (n.d.) *Arkivverket*; accessed September 3, 2013

Lawrence, Mark Atwood (2008) *The Vietnam War. A Concise International History.* Oxford / New York: Oxford University Press

Leif, Thomas (1990) *Die strategische (Ohn-)macht der Friedensbewegung.* Opladen: Westdeutscher Verlag

Leif, Thomas (2001) *Themen und Strategien im Spannungsfeld von basisdemokratischem Anspruch und Spektren-Interessen. Die Friedensbewegung der achtziger Jahre.* www.friedenskooperative.de/netzwerk/histo008.htm [2.6.2012]

Liebknecht, Karl P. A. F. 1973. *Militarism and anti-militarism, with special regard to the International Young Socialist Movement,* New York, Garland Pub. (Der deutsche Text kann im Internet eingesehen werden: www.marxists.org/deutsch/archiv/liebknechtk/1907/mil-antimil/ [2.6.2012]

Lindorfer, Simone (2009) ‚Frauen zwischen Opferstatus und Pragmatismus'. In: Evangelisches- Missionswerk in Deutschland (Hrsg.) 2009, S. 29-34

Lofland, John and Marullo, Sam (1990) 'Introduction: Social Science and Peace Action in the Eighties'. In: Marullo & Lofland 1990, S. 1-16

MacDougall, John (1990), 'Congress and the Campaign to Stop the MX Missile'. In: Marullo & Lofland 1990, S. 180-190

Magnusson, Leif (1988) *Fredskämpen : en bok om Klas Pontus Arnoldson : den förste svensk som fick Nobels fredspris,* Tumba, Stift. Sveriges invandrarinstitut och museum

Martin, Brian (2011) *Backfire Manual. Tactics against Injustice.* www.bmartin.cc/pubs/12bfm/12bfm.pdf [2.6.2012]

Marullo, Sam and Lofland, John (Hrsg.) (1990) *Peace Action in the Eighties. Social Science Perspectives.* Brunswick / London: Rutgers

McGovern, George (1992) ‚Foreword'. In: Small und Hoover (Hrsg.) 1992: xi-xiii

McReynolds, David (1992) ‚Pacifists and the Vietnam Antiwar Movement'. In: Small and Hoover (Hrsg.) 1992: 53-70

Meyer, David S. (1999) 'How the Cold War Was Really Won: The Effects of the Antinuclear- Movements of the 1980s.' In: Giugni, Marco, McAdam, Doug and Tilly, Charles (Hrsg.) *How Social Movements Matter.* Minneapolis/London: University of Minnesota Press, S. 182-203

Meyrowitz, Elliott L. and Campbell, Kenneth J. (1992)'Vietnam Veterans and War Crimes Hearings'. In: Small and Hoover (Hrsg.) 1992, S. 129-140

Moser-Puangsuwan, Yeshua and Weber, Thomas (Hrsg.) (2000) *Nonviolent Intervention Across Borders. A Recurrent Vision.* Honolulu: Spark M. Matsunaga Institute for Peace

Moyer, Bill (1987*) The Movement Action Plan. A Strategic Framework Describing the Eight States of Successful Social Movements.* http://historyisaweapon.com/defcon1/moyermap.html [28.7.2013]

Muller, Jean-Marie (1999b) 'Rétrouver les chemins de la paix.' In: Non-Violence Actualité No 236, June, 11

Myhre, Jan Eivind (2012) *Norsk historie 1814-1905 å byggje ein stat og skape ein nasjon,* Oslo, Det norske samlaget

Nepstad, Sharon Erickson (2011) *Nonviolent Revolutions. Civil Resistance in the Late 20th Century.* Oxford: Oxford University Press

Nielsen, Yngvar (1906) *Norge i 1905 : med en indledende oversigt over unionshistoriens niti aar,* Horten

Nilsson, Torbjörn & Sørensen, Øystein (edsHrsg.) (2005) *1905 -- unionsupplösningens år : nya perspektiv på ett svensk-norskt drama.* Stockholm: Carlsson

Nordlund, K. (1905) *The Swedish-Norwegian union crisis a history with documents*, Upsala. Almqvist & Wiksell

Oelerich, Thomas (2013) '„solidarisch?" Gedanken zum Motto der diesjährigen Ökumenischen FriedensDekade', in: Friedensforum 4/2013, S. 10–11

Ottosen, Morton N. (2005) *"Angreb kan tænkes rettet baade fra Land- og fra Søsiden" -- Militære tiltak og vurderinger i Trøndelag 1890-1905.* MA, University of Oslo

Overy, Bob (1982) *How Effective are Peace Movements?* Montreal: Harvest House

Paffenholz, Thania (2010) ,What Civil Society Can Contribute to Peacebuilding', .In: Paffenholz, Thania (Hrsg.) (2010) *Civil Society and Peacebuilding: A Critical Assessment.* Boulder:Lynne Rienner Publishers, S. 381-404

Peace, Roger (2012) *A Call to Conscience. The Anti-Contra War Campaign.* Amherst and Boston: University of Massachusetts Press

Pentz, Mike (1984) ,Das nukleare Wettrüsten – eine neue Initiative ist jetzt dringend notwendig'. Wissenschaft & Frieden 2/1984, www.wissenschaft-und-frieden.de/seite.php?artikelID=0576 [2.6.2012]

Peterson, Jon (2011) 'Peace Through Strength or Strength Through Peace? The Reagan Administration and the Nuclear Freeze Movement in 1982.' Eras, Edition 12, Issue 2, March 2011, pp. 1-32, http://arts.monash.edu.au/publications/eras/edition-12-issue-2/articles/jpeterson.pdf [12.6.2014]

Pilisuk, Marc and Gaddy, Ellen (2012) ,Against So Much Money and Power, Can the Peace Movement Succeed?', .In: Pilisuk, Marc and Nagler, Michael N. (Hrsg.) (2011) *Peace Movements Worldwide*, Vol. 1, S. 236-254

Raschke, Joachim (1988) *Soziale Bewegungen. Ein historisch-systematischer Grundriß.* Frankfurt / New York: Campus Verlag

Rehn, Elisabeth and Sirleaf, Ellen Johnson (2002) *Women. War. Peace. The Independent Expert's Assessment on the Impact of Armed Conflict on Women and Women's Role in Peace-building.* New York: UNIFEM

Rieker, Heinrich (2007) *Nicht schießen, wir schießen auch nicht! Versöhnung von Kriegsgegnern im Niemandsland 1914–18 und 1939–1945.* Bremen: Donat

Risse-Kappen, Thomas (1988) *Null-Lösung, Entscheidungsprozesse zu den Mittelstreckenwaffen 1970 – 1987.* Frankfurt / New York: Campus Verlag. Hier verwendet wurde die englische Übersetzung: *The Zero Option. INF, West Germany, and Arms Control.* Boulder / London: Westview Press, 1988

Risse-Kappen, Thomas (1995) 'Vom Ost-West-Konflikt zur internationalen Unübersichtlichkeit'. In: Risse-Kappen, Thomas; Wehling, Hans-Georg (Red.) (1995) *Sicherheitspolitik unter geänderten weltpolitischen Rahmenbedingungen.* Stuttgart u. a.: Kohlhammer, S. 10–25

Roberts, Adam (2011) ‚Introduction', .In: Roberts & Ash (Hrsg.) (2011), S. 1-24

Roberts, Adam und Ash, Timothy Garton (Hrsg..) (2011²) *Civil Resistance and Power Politics. The Experience of Nonviolent Action from Gandhi to the Present.* Oxford: Oxford University Press

Roggenbuck, Beate (1991) ‚Just say no – U.S.-Golfkriegsverweigerer vor Gericht'. In: Friedensforum 5/1991, S. 3

Rohwedder, Jörg (2010) ‚Von gespaltenen Eliten und auslösenden Ereignissen'. In: Friedensforum 1/2010, S. 26

Rosenbrock, Christine (2007) *Liberia.* AKUF Kriege-Archiv. www.sozialwiss.uni-hamburg.de/publish/Ipw/Akuf/kriege/260_liberia.htm [20.4.2012]

Rucht, Dieter (2007) 'Engagement in sozialen Bewegungen. Voraussetzungen, Formen, Wirkungen.' In: Kolb, Felix (Hrsg.) *Damit sich was bewegt.* Hamburg:VSA Verlag, S.13–44

Rudolf, Peter und Schaller, Christian (2012) *Targeted Killing – Zur völkerrechtlichen, ethischen und strategischen Problematik gezielten Tötens in der Terrorismus- und Aufstandsbekämpfung.* SWP Studie S1 . Berlin: SWP

Schlichte, Klaus (2002) *Liberia.* AKUF Kriege-Archiv. www.sozialwiss.uni-hamburg.de/publish/Ipw/Akuf/kriege/168_liberia.htm [20.4.2012]

Schlupp-Hauck, Wolfgang (2005) ‚Entwicklungen in der deutschen Anti-Atomwaffen-Bewegung', in: Friedensforum 1/2005, www.friedenskooperative.de/ff/ff05/1-63.htm [2.9.2013]

Schock, Kurt (2005) *Unarmed Insurrections. Peopel Power Movements in Nondemocracies.* Minneapolis:University of Minnesota Press

Schreiber, E. M. (1976) ‚Antiwar demonstrations and American public opinion on the war in Vietnam'. In: British Journal of Sociology Vol 27, No 2, June 1976, S. 225-236

Schweitzer, Christine (2010) *Strategies of Intervention in Protracted Violent Conflicts by Civil Society Actors. The Example of Interventions in the Violent Conflicts in the Area of Former Yugoslavia, 1990–2002.* Vehrte: Soziopublishing. (Dissertation) Herunterzuladen bei: www.ifgk.de/oben/publikationen_all.htm [12.8.2012]

Shapiro, Herbert (1989) 'The Vietnam War and the American Historical Profession'. In: Dumbrell 1989: 7-33

Short, Anthony (1989) 'Vietnam: Alternative Scripts.' In: Dumbrell 1989: 34-42

Singe, Martin (2003) ‚Erste juristische Erfolge für Airbase-Blockierer'. In: Friedensforum 4/2003, S. 3–4

Small, Melvin (1984) ‚The Impact of the Antiwar Movement on Lyndon Johnson, 1965-68: A Preliminary Report'. In: Peace and Change Vol X, No 1, Spring, S. 1-22

Small, Melvin (1996) *Democracy and Diplomacy. The Impact of Domestic Politics on U.S. Foreign Policy, 1789–1994.* Baltimore / London: The John Hopkins University Press

Small, Melvin and Hoover, William D. (Hrsg.) (1992) *Give Peace a Chance. Exploring the Vietnam Antiwar Movement.* New York: Syracuse Press

Sørensen, Øystein (2005) Vad kunde ha hänt? In: Nilsson & Sørensen (Hrsg.) 2005: p. 25-30

Stay, Jochen (2003) ‚Die Kampagne "resist"'. Friedensforum 1/2003, S. 24–25

Stay, Jochen (2005) ‚Wo Recht zu Unrecht wird. Ziviler Ungehorsam in der Anti-AKW-Bewegung:. In: Friedensforum 5/2004

Stephan, Maria J. and Chenoweth, Erica (2008) 'Why Civil Resistance Works. The Strategic Logic of Nonviolent Conflict'. In: International Security, Jg. 33, H. 33-1, S. 7–44

Sternstein, Wolfgang (2013) *„Atomkraft nein danke!" Der lange Weg zum Ausstieg.* Brandes & Apsel. Frankfurt a. M.

Stortinget. (1951) „De hemmelige møter i Stortinget 1905", Oslo

Stråth, Bo (2005) *Union och demokrati : de förenade rikena Sverige och Norge 1814-1905,* Nora, Nya Doxa

Strutynski, Peter (2007) „„Die Mehrheit der Bevölkerung lehnt diesen Einsatz ab"". In: Junge Welt 4. Juli 2007 (Beilage), www.ag-friedensforschung.de/regionen/Afghanistan/strutynski4.html [2.6.2012]

Swerdlow, Amy (1992) 'Not My Son, Not Your Son, Not Their Sons'. Mothers Against the Vietnam Draft'. In: Small and Hoover (Hrsg.) 1992: 159-170

Tempel, Konrad (2010) ‚Eine andere Welt ist möglich'. In: Friedensforum 1/2010, S. 23–25

Terjesen, Bjørn (2001) *Vi skiltes i fred: oppløsningen av den norsk-svenske unionen i 1905,* Oslo, Universitetsforl.

Thorkildsen, Dag (2005) ‚Kyrkan och 1905'. In: Nilsson & Sørensen (Hrsg.) 2005: 181-204

Tilly, Charles (1999) ‚From Interactions to Outcomes in Social Movements'. In: Giugni, Marco, McAdam, Doug and Tilly, Charles (Hrsg.) *How Social Movements Matter.* Minneapolis/London: University of Minnesota Press, S. 253-270

United Nations (2012) *UNMIL. United Nations Mission in Liberia.* www.un.org/en/peacekeeping/missions/unmil/ 26.4.2012]

Wasmuht, Ulrike C. (1987) *Friedensbewegungen der 80er Jahre.* Gießen: Focus

Weibull, Jörgen (1962) *Inför unionsupplösningen 1905 : konsulatfrågan,* Stockholm, Norstedt

Wells, Tom (1994) *The War Within. America's Battle over Vietnam.* Berkeley u. a.: University of California Press

William R. Berkowitz (1973) ‚The Impact of Anti-Vietnam Demonstrations Upon national Public Opinion and Military Indicators', Soc. Sci. Res., vol 2, no 1 (march 1973), S. 1-14

Wittich, Dietmar (2002) *Anhaltender Krieg und bleibende Skepsis. Spärliche Informationen, markige Sprüche und geteilte Meinungen in der Öffentlichkeit.* www.ag-friedensforschung.de/themen/Medien/wittich.html [2.6.2012]

Wittner, Lawrence S. (1984) *Rebels Against War. The American Peace Movement, 1941–1984.* Philadelphia: Temple University Press

Wittner, Lawrence S. (2007) ‚A Short History of Peace Action'. In: Stassen, Glen Harold und Wittner, Lawrence S. (Hrsg.) (2007) *Peace Action. Past, Present and Future.* Boulder / London: Paradigm, S. 1–13

Wolke, Lars Ericson (1999) Plikten framför allt. *Populär Historia*

Wolke, Lars Ericson (2004) Svenska knektar : indelta soldater, ryttare och båtsmän i krig och fred, Lund, Historiska media.

Wolke, Lars Ericson (2004) *Svenska knektar : indelta soldater, ryttare och båtsmän i krig och fred,* Lund, Historiska media.

Zaborowski, Marcin (2009) ‚How did the Wall fall?' ISS Analysis. www.iss.europa.eu/uploads/media/MZ_How_did_the_Wall_fall.pdf [2.6.2012]

Ziemann, Benjamin (2008) 'Situating Peace Movements in the Political Culture of the Cold War. Introduction'. In: Ziemann, Benjamin (Hrsg.) (2008) *Peace Movements in Western Europe, Japan and the USA during the Cold War.* Essen: Klartext, S. 11-38

Zunes, Stephan (2011) ‚The 1991 Gulf War and Aftermath'. In: Pilisuk, Marc and Nagler, Michael N. (Hrsg.) (2011) *Peace Movements Worldwide*, Vol. 2, S. 354-367

Zur Hölle mit dem Teufel – Frauen für ein freies Liberia. Film von Gini Reticker und Abigail Disney, Begleitheft. Siehe auch: Film: www.praythedevilbacktohell.com/v3/ [24.4.2012]

www.ingramcontent.com/pod-product-compliance
Lightning Source LLC
LaVergne TN
LVHW010926110826
845149LV00013B/2490

* 9 7 8 9 1 8 8 0 6 1 1 2 6 *